WOMEN'S
BASKETBALL

Dr. James Naismith

WOMEN'S BASKETBALL

MARY M. BELL

Northern Illinois University

Second Edition

ⱳcb
WM. C. BROWN COMPANY PUBLISHERS
Dubuque, Iowa

PHYSICAL EDUCATION

Consulting Editor
Aileene Lockhart
University of Southern California

PARKS AND RECREATION

Consulting Editor
David Gray
California State College, Long Beach

HEALTH

Consulting Editor
Robert Kaplan
Ohio State University

This book is dedicated to Jeaners and Paula and to many other former students who love to play. They have given of themselves to their team-mates, their schools, and me. I am very grateful.

KEY TO DIAGRAMS

$\oplus$ = Defensive player

$\bigcirc$ = Offensive player

⟶ = Path of player

- - - - ▶ = Path of ball

╫╫╫╫╫╫ = Dribble

) = Screen

⌐ = Pivot

Contents

Preface

Basketball for women has developed into a much more challenging and complex game in the last few years. The change to the five player, full court game has stimulated greater interest and enjoyment to both players and spectators. It has, however, necessitated new patterns of offensive and defensive play and created a need for more information.

This book is written with the hope that it will help both teachers and coaches provide the best instruction possible. In order for students to gain the greatest enjoyment from their participation, they need to know more than the basic skills of the game. They must have some understanding of offensive and defensive strategy. Full understanding of the game will also increase their enjoyment and appreciation as spectators of the wonderful American game of basketball.

The chapters on defensive play precede those on offensive play because it is the author's belief that offense must be taught in relation to the defense it will attack. Hence, in instructing both beginning classes and interscholastic teams, it is suggested that team defensive play should be taught before offensive play.

Acknowledgments

The author is grateful to the many people who assisted in the preparation of this book: Harry Herbert and Barry Stark for the photography; Douglas Keaton, Concordia Teachers College, and the DeKalb High School, for the use of the uniforms; Northern Illinois University, for its assistance in obtaining library materials and photographs; the students, Mary Ellen Bajec, Sue Blotch, Patsy Box, Ruth Dodd, Ruth Fender, Judy Hix, Karen Judge, Chris LoMonaco, Carolyn Newland, Linda Oster, Bonnie Parkhouse, and Kathy Totel, for their pictorial demonstrations; Springfield College, for the picture of Dr. Naismith; and Lou Jean Moyer, for her help with the preparation of the manuscript.

History and Values of Basketball

Basketball was first played in the late fall of 1891 at Springfield College in Springfield, Massachusetts. The game grew from the imagination and inventiveness of Dr. James Naismith, an instructor at the college. Naismith worked under Dr. Luther Gulick and was assigned by Dr. Gulick to develop a new game that could be played indoors.

Wanting to avoid the rough play of soccer and football, Naismith placed the goal above the players' heads. When he requested two boxes to nail to the balcony, he received two peach baskets. The baskets not only made satisfactory goals but also gave the game its name. The baskets were fastened to the balcony which was ten feet above the floor. This is still the regulation height for the baskets.

Many new regulations have been added to Naismith's original thirteen and changes in the rules have been paralleled by changes in equipment. At first players used a soccer ball and scored when the ball was shot into and stayed in the basket. A retriever stationed in the balcony returned the ball to play. In cases where it was necessary to attach the baskets to a wall instead of a balcony, the retriever had to use a ladder to recover the ball. The first woven wire baskets which were manufactured had no opening at the bottom and it was several years before the baskets were constructed to allow the ball to drop through to the floor.

Basketball immediately appealed to both men and women. Within two weeks after the first game at Springfield College, a group of young women teachers from a nearby school asked to play. The first game for college women was played at Smith College under the direction of Senda Berensen. By 1899 the first rules for women were written,

1

and by 1905 a permanent basketball rules committee was established. Since 1899, basketball for women has become much faster, demanding much skill and endurance.

In the early game the court was divided into three sections with players permitted to play in just one area. The three court game was a chance happening and occurred because of a misunderstanding. Miss Clara Baer of Newcomb College in New Orleans saw a diagram of the 1893 rules which showed dotted lines across the court in two places. The lines were intended as a guide for the positioning of players but Miss Baer interpreted them to be restraining lines; thus, the three court game developed for women with two guards, two forwards, and two centers. In 1938 the game was changed to three forwards and three guards with the center line a boundary, but it wasn't until 1971 that the women adopted the 5 player, full court game, which has proved very popular.

There has been a phenomenal growth in the popularity of basketball as a spectator sport in the United States. Recent estimates indicate that 138,000,000 fans watch high school and college basketball games each season. Many a small town has built a high school gymnasium that seats more than the total population of the community. Such facts indisputably indicate that basketball is popular as a spectator sport and offers genuine recreational value to millions.

Since World War II basketball has developed tremendously as an international sport. It is beginning to rival soccer as the leading sport on the international scene. The game is regulated by the Federation Internationale de Basketball Amateur which represents more than 120 nations. Basketball made its initial appearance in the Olympic Games in 1936 in Berlin when competition was opened to men, but women's basketball was to be delayed for forty years.

Although basketball provides recreation to millions of spectators, the greatest values are to those who participate as players. There are many personal benefits derived from competing in basketball. This is true whether a person plays in a backyard pick-up game, in a required physical education class, in an intramural or recreational league, or in a highly competitive conference.

Physical Values

The importance of vigorous physical activity in maintaining a healthy body has long been recognized. Physical exercise contributes to a woman's general strength, health, beauty, and coordination. Although extreme muscular strength is not desirable for a woman in American culture, a woman should be able to engage in a normal day's activities and still be capable of enjoying an evening of recreational bowling or dancing. Strength sufficient to hold the body in good alignment with strong abdominal and back muscles will make a woman feel better as well as add to her attractiveness.

More important than general strength is the role physical activity plays in health. Since increasing evidence indicates a relationship between the level of physical activity and the health of the cardiovascular system, conditioning may be a protection against heart disease. Regular physical activity reduces problems of overweight and obesity. The prevention of obesity reduces a woman's susceptibility to degenerative disease, especially in her later life. Physical exercise increases longevity in other ways such as developing the ability to adapt in an emergency situation with reserve capacity, which may mean avoiding accidental disability or death.

As well as improving health, regular exercise aids in the preservation of the physical characteristics of youth. A woman feels better and is more attractive if she is not overweight and if she stands erect without strain.

Another physical benefit derived from participation in a sport such as basketball is improved coordination. A player acquires grace and beauty of movement in perfecting a hook shot or other skillful maneuvers required in playing the game. Many fundamental movements such as running, stopping, changing direction, throwing, catching and jumping, essential in a game of basketball, are repeated over and over. With repeated practice come body control, balance, and a sense of timing and rhythm.

Mental and Emotional Values

A basketball player must make instantaneous decisions. Although these decisions are made during the excitement of the game, the player must remain calm and poised, her temper under control. By showing disgust or irritation with another person or herself, a player loses the respect of the group. An angry or irritated player is less effective than one who retains self-control in the face of frustrating circumstances. Sometimes the beginning player reacts to the difficult situation with bewilderment, or a "rattled" player throws the ball away and commits errors in technique and judgment. As a player becomes more experienced, however, she makes split-second decisions with confidence and good judgment.

While participating in a vigorous sport such as basketball, the player releases emotional tension, and by giving her complete attention in a challenging game, she temporarily discards the stresses of living. This ability to become fully absorbed in a game frees her from daily cares and leaves her feeling refreshed. Meanwhile her aggressions and hostilities are released through vigorous activity which is socially acceptable. In addition, physical activity has a beneficial effect on the body's ability to withstand stress because repeated exercise improves the stress adaptation mechanism of the body and less adjustment is necessary. The player not only releases hostility but also withstands stress with ease.

Social Values

Much has been written about the contribution of sports to social adjustment and evidence supports the claim that those individuals who have participated successfully in athletics tend to be better adjusted socially and more capable of leadership than those who have had little experience in athletics. However, there is little evidence that their success is the result of their athletic participation. Persons who seek athletic participation may do so because they already have traits of dominance and social acceptability. Research indicates that high motor ability scores and social adjustment scores may be significantly related.

Teachers and coaches who help girls and young women to improve their coordination and to compete successfully in basketball give these young people opportunities to develop socially. Being members of a team satisfies the innate desire to belong and develops a feeling of self-worth. Being on a team gives opportunities for meeting new people and making friends. If the team represents a school or club and plays teams from other institutions, the players learn how to act as guests and hostesses.

Recreational Values

Basketball as a leisure time activity can be a source of enjoyment to both a participant and a spectator. Many groups, such as the YWCA, AAU, a park district, or a church, sponsor basketball leagues for young women who are no longer students. It is necessary to remember that though some people overlook the role of play in the lives of adults, recreational activities are important to adults. The psychiatrist, Dr. William Menninger, writes, "There is considerable scientific evidence that the healthy personality is one who not only plays, but who takes his play seriously,"[1] and ". . . the most constructive and beneficial play is something that has to be learned and is not likely to be an accidental ability or an inherited trait. . . . For maximum satisfaction, one requires not only encouragement but almost always some instruction. . . . An effective community recreation program is just as important to mental health as sanitation is to physical health."[2]

Ethical Values

Sportsmanship has long been hailed as one of the concomitant learnings of physical education and athletics. Playing basketball can be a factor in developing moral attitudes in young people. Although one does not have to look to the intercollegiate basketball scandals to realize that this is not always so, there are many opportunities in the game which lend themselves to the building of character. A girl needs to feel that she is contributing to something greater than her own self-interests. To do the best that she can for the sake of her team can be a very rewarding experience. Placing the good of the team above her separate desires may be a real lesson in selflessness. Whether or not she develops such character traits depends largely upon the leaders of her group.

Responsibility of the Teacher

The values that accrue to the participant of basketball are far more important than her success in being able to put the ball in the basket. If she has little success, however, her participation will be very limited and there may be few resultant benefits. Acquisition of skill and understanding is important, but it is not the main purpose of participation. If teachers and coaches have a firm belief that the game is not as important as what happens to the individual players, they must have a good understanding of the contributions that basketball is able to

1. William C. Menninger, "Recreation and Mental Health," *Recreation*, Nov. 1948, p. 343.
2. *Ibid.*, p. 346.

give to the players. Furthermore, it is the responsibility of teachers or coaches to communicate these convictions to the players.

REFERENCES

1. Bell, Mary M. "Measurement of Selected Outcomes of Participation in Girls' High School Interscholastic Basketball," Unpublished Dissertation, State University of Iowa, 1955.
2. Cowell, Charles C. "The Contributions of Physical Activity to Social Development," *Research Quarterly of the American Association for Health, Physical Education, and Recreation,* May, 1960, Part II.
3. *Encyclopædia Britannica, Inc.* Chicago: William Benton Publisher, 1969.
4. Healey, William. *High School Basketball, Coaching, Managing, Administering.* Danville, Ill.: The Interstate Printers and Publishers, Inc., 1962.
5. Hein, Fred V., and Ryan, Allen J. "The Contributions of Physical Activity to Physical Health," *Research Quarterly of the American Association for Health, Physical Education, and Recreation,* May, 1960, Part II.
6. Lawrence, Helen, and Fox, Grace. *Basketball for Girls and Women.* New York: McGraw-Hill Book Co., Inc., 1954.
7. Menninger, William C. "Recreation and Mental Health," *Recreation,* Nov., 1948.
8. Merriman, J. Burton. "Relationship of Personality Traits to Motor Ability," *Research Quarterly of the American Association for Health, Physical Education, and Recreation,* May, 1960, Part I.
9. Michael, Ernest D. Jr. "Stress Adaptation through Exercise," *Research Quarterly of the American Association for Health, Physical Education, and Recreation,* March, 1957.
10. Naismith, James. *Basketball, Its Origin and Development.* New York: Association Press, 1941.
11. Scott, M. Gladys. "The Contributions of Physical Activity to Psychological Development," *Research Quarterly of the American Association for Health, Physical Education, and Recreation,* May, 1960, Part II.
12. Sperling, Abraham P. "The Relationship Between Personality Adjustment and Achievement in Physical Education Activities," *Research Quarterly of the American Association for Health, Physical Education, and Recreation,* Oct., 1942.
13. Steinhaus, Arthur H. *Toward An Understanding of Health and Physical Education.* Dubuque, Iowa: Wm. C. Brown Company Publishers, 1963.

Defensive Skills

Since a team plays defensively about fifty percent of the time, defensive techniques must be explained, demonstrated, and practiced with just as much emphasis as the offensive skills of ball handling and shooting. This chapter is devoted to a description of the proper techniques for footwork, use of hands, positioning, rebounding, and aggressiveness. In each case common errors are listed, proper coaching points are indicated, and drills for each skill are described.

Footwork

The player assumes a slight crouch with the weight on the balls of the feet but with the heels on the floor. The feet in a side stride position are spread slightly greater than the width of the shoulders. One foot is 6 to 10 inches ahead of the other. The player should move with a short, sliding step, without crossing the feet.

It is important that the player is balanced yet can react instantly to movements by the opponent. When guarding an opponent in possession of the ball, the defensive player must be alert to the threat of a drive. The guard is at a disadvantage because she cannot start moving until after the opponent begins an offensive attack. If the opponent starts to dribble to the guard's right, the guard should step backward, *not* sideward, with the right foot. The same backward movement with the left foot is used if the opponent drives to the guard's left.

Guarding Stance

The defensive player should come to understand that it is easier to start backward with the rear foot; thus, this becomes her strong side and the forward foot her weak side in attempting to thwart a drive or cut by an opponent. When guarding an opponent the player should learn to place her feet in such a way that her strength is where it is most needed. Players should learn to feel comfortable with either foot forward.

The inside foot forward and the outside foot to the rear is considered the proper defensive position of the feet. The inside foot is the one nearer to an imaginary line drawn between the two baskets and the outside foot is closer to the side boundary line. This foot alignment of the defensive player places the more vulnerable side toward the middle where the area is more congested and where teammates should be available for assistance. With the outside foot to the rear the defensive player is better positioned to defend against a drive to the outside because she can force the dribbler to the sidelines. Sound defensive play attempts the forcing of the play away from the middle area toward the sidelines.

Another defensive concept is helpful when the opponent has approached the sideline or the end lines. The defensive player should learn to make use of the boundary lines to her advantage. Since the offensive player needs space in order to maneuver, the defensive player would like to reduce the space available to her opponent. Leading with the foot which is nearer the boundary line gives the opponent less space to the outside.

Common Errors

1. Player's body too erect; no bend in the knees.
2. Player has too much flexion at the hips.
3. Player's weight on one foot rather than on both.
4. Player takes first step sideward rather than backward in attempting to stop a driving opponent.
5. Player fails to move feet and tries to reach with arm in attempting to stop a driving opponent.

Coaching Points

1. Body weight should be balanced with head up and knees relaxed.
2. First movement should be back and then sideward to stop a driving opponent.
3. Players must stay mentally alert one hundred per cent of the time so they can react instantly to an opponent's movement.
4. Players should learn the concept that a player guards with her feet.

Drills

1. Spread formation; all players assume guarding stance in side-by-side position and face leader. Leader moves with guarding step and group changes direction as leader changes hers. Instead of using changes in position, leader may signal with whistle or arm movement.
2. With small numbers of students, players may work in couples without using a ball. Offensive player uses running step to get inside defensive player. Guarding player practices defensive footwork and attempts to prevent opponent from getting inside.
3. Players run short races running backwards.
4. Players form single file lines with a large space in front of them. First player turns around and assumes a defensive position facing the second player. Player No. 2 has the ball and, using a dribble, attempts to drive around the defensive player. When practicing footwork, the defensive players keep their arms at their sides, forcing them to use their feet. When the players turn around to return to the line, the offensive and defensive players trade places. (Twenty-five or thirty feet should separate the lines for this drill.)

5. One-on-one. X_1 passes the ball to O_1 and moves out to guard her. O_1 may dribble or shoot over X_1. X_1 should go to within three or four feet of O_1 in order to block a shot and O_1 should be encouraged to drive if possible. Players go to the end of the opposite line and the ball is passed to X_2. (See Figure 1.)

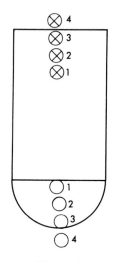

Figure 1

Use of Hands

A defensive player guarding an opponent who has the ball should keep one hand over the ball and the other out to the side at waist height. The fingers should be comfortably spread and the palms of the hands toward the ball. If the left foot is forward, the left hand should be over the ball; if the right foot is forward the right hand should cover the ball. This gives the player a greater reach as well as better balance. When a defensive player is moving to her right to stop a driving opponent, the right hand should be out to the side in a position to intercept or deflect the ball. If the defensive player attempts to steal the ball from a dribbler, the hand movement should be upward in order to prevent fouling.

The defensive player may drop both hands to waist or hip height when the opponent starts a drive, but she should bring one hand up immediately as the opponent stops. The hand that is up covering the ball is in a position to obscure the opponent's vision as well as to block a shot or pass. The defensive player should always be alert to the possibility of tieing the ball. The guard should make maximum effort to block or deflect shots and should jump with an opponent who has left her feet in an attempt to score. If the opponent shoots with the right hand, the guard should use the right hand in attempting to block the shot.

Common Errors
1. Defensive player fails to cover ball with hand.
2. Lack of aggressiveness with hands. Guard gives up too soon in attempting to block shot.
3. Defensive player uses poor judgment in attempting to steal ball and commits a hacking foul.

Coaching Points
1. Ball should be covered with one hand, but not two. The other hand should be used to stop a drive.
2. Defensive player should *never* give up but instead attempt to block every shot.

Drills
1. Drills 1, 4, and 5 under defensive footwork.
2. Three students using one ball. Two defensive players attempt to tie the ball. The offensive player may pivot and move the ball but may not dribble.

Positioning

A good defensive position is between the opponent and the basket. A defensive player should be extremely careful about pulling out of this position, for if a defensive player has lost position, she has nothing. Maintaining a good defensive position is the all important requirement in defensive play.

Guarding an Opponent Without the Ball

A good defensive player must learn to be alert and aggressive all of the time. Too often inexperienced players tend to relax slightly as they cease to guard a player with the ball. An aggressive defensive player will force his opponent into moving out of his normal receiving zone and will make the offensive player work just to receive the ball. This will cause poorer angles of reception and possible passing lanes and less desirable shots. The offensive player has to face the problem of adjusting to playing a style of game that is not the desirable one for her. This is a great psychological hazard for some players and they tend to panic or to try too hard.

The defensive player must learn to watch both the player without the ball and the ball simultaneously. She should avoid turning her head back and forth but develop the ability to see all of the play. Focusing on the midpoint between the ball and the player and developing peripheral vision is important. As the defensive player's distance from the ball increases she should float toward the ball and play a slightly looser defensive position. This gives her more time to adjust to movements by the opposition and puts her in a better position to come to the aid of a teammate. This also puts her in a better position to combat the screen.

Although a defensive player who is guarding a player without the ball will be in a slightly more erect position than one who is guarding a player in possession of the ball, the knees must remain somewhat flexed. A defensive player should never allow her knees to stiffen as this causes quick movements to become much more difficult. Stiffening of the knees is a sign of weariness.

Guarding an Opponent in Possession of the Ball

When guarding an opponent who is in possession of the ball, the defensive player should remember several things:

1. When the opponent is far from the basket, play her more loosely than when she is near the basket.
2. When the opponent has not yet dribbled, give her three to four feet to prevent her from driving. If she has dribbled, move in closer.
3. Do not leave the floor to block a shot unless certain that the opponent is not faking a shot.
4. Attempt to force an opponent into the least dangerous path. If an opponent starts to drive from the head of the circle, force her toward the sideline or take her to the base line, but keep her away from the basket. If an opponent in the corner starts to drive for the basket, keep her to the inside or away from the base line. Forcing her to the inside will probably move her into an area where other defensive players will be able to stop her. If the opponent drives past the guard on the base line side, she will often be wide open with no defensive player in a position to guard her.
5. Study the movements of the opponents. Observe their methods of shooting and driving, and their patterns of play. Learn to anticipate.

6. Focus on the waist of the opponent. She may fake with her eyes or the ball but rarely her midsection.

Player Outnumbered by Opponents

Defensive positioning is very important when the player is outnumbered by the opponents. The defensive player should never be drawn away from the basket but should allow a long shot rather than permit a pass to go behind her for a lay-up attempt.

Defense Against the Screen

Defensive positioning when opponents are attempting a screen often creates serious problems. Defensive players should watch movements of opposing players and anticipate the screen. An alert defensive player can often prevent successful screens by moving away from the screener before she can gain a screening position. If a screen is made, the defensive player should make every effort to break it. Too often players resign themselves to having been taken out of a play and make no effort to combat the screen. An aggressive, determined defensive player can quickly move around the screening player and be in a position to guard the ball. Even if the guard is unable to prevent a shot, she may hurry the shooting player, thus causing the shooter to be inaccurate.

Frequently it is wiser to combat the screen by switching opponents than by trying to break the screen. The defensive player who is being screened should not call the switch as she cannot see the entire play. The player guarding the screener is in a position to see the play and calls the switch. When defensive players anticipate switching, they should talk to each other and not change defensive assignments until the call is given.

Guarding a Pivot Player

Although the defensive position is defined as being between the opponent and the opponent's basket, this is not always true. An exception is sometimes made to this rule when guarding a pivot player who is not in possession of the ball. Since every effort should be made to prevent the ball from being passed to the pivot, the defensive player assigned to guard the pivot may play beside or in front of her.

Common Errors

1. Player attempts an interception and loses position.

2. Defensive player jumps when opponent fakes a shot; opponent drives around her.
3. Defensive player makes no effort to break a screen play.

Coaching Points
1. Defensive player should never leave position for a doubtful interception.
2. Guarding player should not jump to block shot unless certain that opponent is shooting.
3. Defensive players should learn to play differently against different opponents. Go out on a good set shooter; stay back for a fast driving opponent.

Drills
1. Numbers 4 and 5 under defensive footwork.
2. Two-on-one. Two players try to move the ball past a defensive player for a lay-up shot. The players should try to move the ball quickly in one or two passes. One player may start to dribble for the basket hoping to draw the defensive player toward her so that she can pass to her cutting teammate. After completing the play, the two players go to the end of the opposite line. (See Figure 2.)
3. Three-on-two. Same as Number 2. One defensive player should play at the free throw line, the other behind her. When the front de-

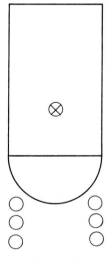

Figure 2

fensive player stops the opponent and the opponent passes, the rear player goes with the pass and the front defensive player drops back toward the basket.

Rebounding

The defensive player should first block her opponent from moving to the basket and then get into a rebounding position. She watches to see which way her opponent will move and then does a rear pivot to that side. The defensive player should take a large step when executing the pivot in order to create a big obstruction to her opponent. She moves slowly toward the basket, blocking the opponent all the way. She must watch the ball and be aware of the angle and the amount of force with which it was thrown. As the defensive player prepares to jump, her feet should be in a wide side stride position. This helps her to block the opponents and gives her a firm base for the jump.

She should time her movement to the basket so that she jumps slightly forward and with a little bend in the hips. This prevents an opponent from reaching over her shoulders to tie the ball. The defensive player flexes ankles, knees, and hips and pushes hard from the balls of the feet. Both arms are thrown upward with a forceful motion, and the player should attain full extension in the body and arms. The player should reach with two hands and come down protecting the ball so it cannot be tied. The player should land with feet spread, in a crouched position, elbows away from the body thus giving added protection to the ball.

Common Errors
1. Player fails to block opponent.
2. Player gets little height in jumping.
3. Player keeps ball overhead and the ball is tied.

Coaching Points
1. Defensive player should watch opponent and anticipate which direction she will go.
2. Player should be in wide side stride position and use vigorous swing of arms to aid in gaining height. (Movement is similar to diving or jumping on a trampoline.)
3. Player should keep back to opponent and crouch with the ball in front of the abdomen. Player may dribble or pass in order to start moving the ball away from the basket.

Drills
1. Drill Number 5 for footwork. Have player try to rebound shot and defensive player attempt to block her from basket.
2. Drills Number 2 and Number 3 for positioning.
3. Have players shooting from anywhere on the floor, one ball for each basket. Only the player who gets the rebound will get to shoot. Players at each basket should be approximately the same height.
4. Three offensive players line up behind the free throw line with three defensive players facing them. One of the offensive players attempts a shot, and the three offensive players try to move inside the guards for the rebound. Each guard tries to block her opponent. This drill should teach blocking out opponents and cooperating with teammates in moving for rebounds.

Aggressiveness

A good defensive player must develop judgment about when she may or may not leave her defensive position, but she must always put pressure on the offensive players. She should harass the opponents with her interceptions, deflections, tie balls, and blocked shots. A defensive player must hurry her opponent and never allow her to get set for shots. Some defensive players are so timid they actually back away from a driving opponent. Other players, in trying to be aggressive, are rough and foul the opponents. To play well defensively, a player must develop not only good judgment but also determination and persistence. This "hustle" or "desire" that is so important in defensive play can be developed through experience, conditioning, and perseverance.

Common Errors
1. Poor judgment about an attempted interception and a resulting foul.
2. Timidity and lack of confidence which result in a "give up" attitude.

Coaching Points
1. A foul is a costly mistake.
2. A player should always attempt to reach her full potential as a player. Learning to do her best regardless of circumstances is of utmost importance to every player.

Drills

1. Drill Number 5 for footwork.
2. Drill Number 3 for positioning.
3. Five-on-five. Half-court game situation, offensive players get points for baskets. Defensive players get points for moving the ball to the center line.

REFERENCES

1. Meyer, Margaret, and Schwarz, Marguerite. *Team Sports for Girls and Women.* Philadelphia: W. B. Saunders Co., 1965.
2. Miller, Donna Mae, and Ley, Katherine. *Individual and Team Sports for Women.* Englewood Cliffs, N. J.: Prentice-Hall, Inc., 1955.
3. Moore, Dudley. "Daring Defense Pays Off." *Sports Illustrated,* Dec. 8, 1958.
4. Neal, Patsy. *Basketball Techniques for Women.* New York: Ronald Press Co., 1966.
5. Newell, Pete, and Benington, John. *Basketball Methods.* New York: Ronald Press Co., 1962.
6. Rupp, Adolph. *Championship Basketball.* Englewood Cliffs, N. J.: Prentice-Hall, Inc., 1957.
7. Wooden, John R. *Practical Modern Basketball.* New York: Ronald Press Co., 1966.

Chapter 3

Offensive Skills

Mastery of the beginning offensive skills, especially catching and passing, is necessary for playing basketball. Ball control is essential in building any offensive attack. Since drills for the development of catching and throwing often become monotonous, it is important that the teacher or coach plan a progression of challenging drills. The plan should include an element of game play. When working on a "feed" pass, for example, a pivot player should be used to "feed" to a player cutting for the basket.

Catching

In catching any object, the body must absorb the shock of impact produced by the momentum of the thrown object. The greater the weight and speed of the object, the greater the impact and the greater the problem of control and possible injury to the receiver. Players should be taught to reduce the shock of impact by gradually reducing the speed of the ball. In basketball this is commonly called "give." When receiving the ball, the hands and body should be relaxed. The arms reach to receive the ball and move back toward the body as the ball is caught. Giving with the ball through as much distance as possible increases the time in which the force is absorbed and brings into use hands, wrists, arms, shoulders, hips, knees, and ankles.

The fingers should be pointed up when the ball is caught above the waist and down when caught below the waist, thus the palms of the hands and not the fingertips are presented to the ball. Players should also be taught to "cup" the hands when catching. This reduces the chances of injury to the fingers. Having the hands cupped when catching puts the ball in a better playing position since the fingers, and not the palms, control the ball. The ball therefore should be caught with the palms only if it comes with great speed.

Players should also be taught to move toward the pass rather than to wait for the ball. All too often the ball is intercepted because a player stands and waits rather than going to meet the ball.

Common Errors

1. Standing still and waiting for the ball.
2. Failure to get the body in line with the ball.
3. Lack of give in catching hard passes.

Coaching Points

1. Move to meet the pass.
2. Move to get the body in line with the ball. This makes catching the ball easier and protects the ball by blocking an opponent to the rear.
3. In giving with the pass, move the ball into position for the next pass.

Passing

The ability to pass accurately will make receiving the ball much easier, and the ability to "thread the needle" or put the ball through an opening creates opportunities for shooting. While it is not necessary for a player to master all the passes, she should be able to execute several. Catching and throwing in one motion is often necessary in a basketball game, and the player should be able to throw from any height. If she receives a high pass or rebound or a pass at chest or hip level, she must be able to throw from this position. As the player gives in receiving the ball, she should be moving the ball into position for the next pass.

Although in some situations the ball should reach the receiver above her head or at hip height, the majority of passes should be aimed at chest height. It is usually desirable for the ball to follow the shortest distance from the passer to receiver. This means that the ball should not be arched but should move in horizontal flight to the receiver. This does not hold true, of course, when it becomes necessary to lob the ball over or bounce it under a defensive player. Players need good peripheral vision so that it is not necessary to look at the receiver as they pass. They must learn to throw ahead of a moving receiver so that the ball can be easily handled when it reaches the receiver.

Chest Pass

This pass is probably the most used pass in basketball. Since the ball is often received chest high, the chest pass can be executed in very little time. The chest pass is delivered from the same position as the chest shot, and the defensive player has a difficult time anticipating plays. This pass is best for a short quick throw and can be executed at top speed. It is, however, a poor long distance pass.

When performing this pass, the player holds the ball with the fingers and thumbs in front of her chest. The thumbs are behind the ball with the fingers pointing forward. The ball is pushed forward with the impetus coming equally from each hand. The power comes from arm extension and wrist snap. For younger players who have difficulty producing power, it may be helpful to suggest using a forward stride position and stepping to shift the body weight forward with the throw. This is preferable to suggesting that the ball be dropped to the waist before throwing in an effort to develop more momentum because this may produce a bad habit which will be difficult to break at a later time.

Common Errors
1. Failure to get full arm extension.
2. Pushing more with one hand than the other.
3. Turning the elbows out away from the body.

Coaching Points
1. Get a complete follow-through with full arm extension. Wrists go from slight hyperextension to extension or slight flexion, and the hands rotate inwardly until the thumbs point downward.
2. Keep the ball close to the chest with the hands at the side of the ball and the thumbs behind the ball.
3. Try to correct "elbows out" by concentrating on hand position. If the fingers point forward and the hands rotate inwardly, it will be very difficult to turn the elbows out.

One Hand Underhand

The movement for this pass is similar to pitching a softball, delivering a bowling ball, or serving a volleyball or shuttlecock. It is useful for a short, low pass and can be used to slip the ball under the arms of a defensive player with her hands in a high position.

Hand Position After Release
of Chest Pass

If the ball is thrown with the right hand, the left foot should be forward. The longer the backswing the greater the momentum. The release is important since, too often, players cup the hand and the ball is lobbed for a weak ineffective pass which can be easily intercepted. The fingers and the hand should extend toward the receiver and the elbow should be straight, thus using the full length of the lever (arm).

Common Errors
1. Using a short arc for the arm swing which fails to develop much momentum.
2. Bending the elbow or cupping the hand, resulting in an arched pass.

Coaching Points
1. Use enough backswing to develop momentum for the distance of the pass. A short pass may require very little backswing. To develop a longer arc, take a step with the forward foot.
2. Keep the ball low by releasing it below the hip.

Two Hand Underhand
This pass can be used for a short low pass when the ball is caught at hip height. It is often used for a "feed" pass or hand off to a player breaking for the basket. The ball is held at the player's side with

the hands on the sides of the ball. The power is developed by the arm swing and by strong abduction of the wrists at the end of the arm swing. This pass is executed most easily if the left foot is forward when passing from the right side of the body. When the pass is used while in a pivot position, with the back to the basket to feed a cutting player, however, it is best to step with the right foot when passing to the right. The right leg is used as a screen in this case.

Common Errors
1. Little force because of weak wrist action or lack of arm extension.
2. Releasing the ball too late, resulting in a lobbed slow pass.

Coaching Points
1. Use the arms and body. Sometimes this is called a shovel pass because of the arm and body action.
2. Keep the fingers reaching at the end of the wrist snap.

One Hand Overhand

This pass is sometimes called the baseball pass because it is executed like an overhand throw. It is used for attaining distance. If the player is throwing with the right hand, the ball is brought behind the right ear and the trunk is rotated to the right so that the left shoulder is pointing toward the target. The weight should be on the right foot and is shifted from the right to the left foot as the trunk rotates to the left. The power thus comes from body action as well as from arm extension and wrist flexion. The ball should be released at head height or above. It is difficult for a closely guarded player to use this pass because a charging foul may result.

Common Errors
1. Lack of power because of failure to bring all body parts into play or to coordinate movements.
2. Lack of accuracy. Long passes are easily intercepted.

Coaching Points
1. Step with the right foot after releasing the ball. This allows for complete weight transfer.
2. Use long passes sparingly and only when the receiver is unguarded.
3. Make a hard straight pass; the slower the pass, the more time for interception.

Two Hand Overhand

This pass can be used after rebounding because the ball is held in a high position. It is also a good pass to get the ball to the pivot player. The ball is held above the head with the hands on the sides of the ball. The arms move forward, and the wrist snap gives the final momentum to the ball.

Common Errors

1. Relying on the arms alone instead of arms and wrists. This practice takes longer to release the pass and is more apt to result in fouling.
2. Holding the ball above the head while preparing to throw. The ball can be tied easily by a defensive player behind the passer.

Coaching Points

1. Use strong adduction of wrists at release.
2. Develop deception and avoid making a slow, obvious pass.

Bounce

This pass can be executed with either one or two hands. It is used to get the ball past the defensive player by sending the ball under her hands. It is a slow pass and often is overused by inexperienced players. The ball should be released at waist or hip height. It should be directed to a spot about three feet in front of the receiver so that it reaches the receiver while still rising. If a high slow bounce is desired for a cutting player, backspin can be imparted to the ball.

Common Errors

1. Causing the ball to bounce eight or ten feet from the receiver resulting in a slow dropping ball which is hard for the receiver to handle and which is easily intercepted.
2. Using a bounce pass when a direct pass would be faster.
3. Throwing the ball into the hand of a guarding player.

Coaching Points

1. Make the ball reach the receiver on the rise.
2. Fake a high throw to get the defensive player to move her hand high.

Two Hand Shoulder

This pass can be useful as a short quick throw from right to left or vice versa. In moving a ball around a zone, a player can use this pass effectively when she receives the ball at the right shoulder from the right and passes to the left. The ball barely hesitates in flight if this pass is well executed. One hand is on top of the ball and the other underneath. If done from right to left, the left hand is on top and the right hand on the bottom of the ball. The movement is in a horizontal plane. The arms extend and the wrists snap at release. Much of the power comes from the adduction of the wrists.

Common Errors
1. Poor hand placement which restricts wrist action.
2. Failure to use wrist snap.

Coaching Points
1. Use strong wrist action.
2. Use body shift of weight. If throwing from right to left, step on the left foot with the release.
3. Move the arms in a horizontal plane.

Hook Pass
This is one of the more difficult passes. It is used when the passer is closely guarded because her body is in position to protect the ball. When the ball is thrown with the right hand, the left shoulder should be pointing toward the receiver. The ball is started with two hands and then can rest against the right forearm at the beginning of the arm swing. The elbow should be extended because the longer the lever, the greater the power. The swing comes from the shoulder; the elbow remains extended as the arm is brought overhead. There is no body rotation; the left shoulder remains pointing toward the receiver, and the head is turned so that the eyes are focused on the receiver. The ball is carried up in the palm of the right hand and is released above the head. The final action at the point of release is flexion of the right hand. The arm does not pass in front of the face but moves toward the right ear so that the ball is released above the head rather than in front of the face. If the ball is carried in front of the face, the defensive player will be able to block it.

The hook pass is often used with a jump. If throwing with the right hand, the player should take the last step with the left foot and should bring the right knee high in order to achieve elevation.

Common Errors
1. Rotating the trunk and bringing the arm in front of the face.

2. Releasing the ball too soon so that wrist flexion is omitted; the ball is sent in an upward arc instead of being directed downward.

Coaching Points
1. Keep the elbow straight as the arm is brought upward.
2. The trunk may bend sideward in the direction of the pass. This keeps the opponent away from the ball.

Drills

These suggested drills do not include those that combine passing with other skills such as the dribble or pivot. They are a beginning progression for the development of ball handling skills. Although it is wise to start with stationary positions in learning catching and throwing, moving patterns should be practiced very early. Players must learn the proper footwork which allows them to handle the ball while moving rapidly without traveling.

Stationary Drills
1. Leader facing single file.
2. Circle formation.
3. Circle formation with two leaders inside. This could be called "Catch Up" ball. The leaders stand back to back, each holding a ball. They throw to each person in succession in the circle; each player returns the ball to the leader. They move both balls the same direction around the circle until one has caught up to the other.
4. One ball to two people (or four or six). Count the number of passes made in 15 seconds.
5. Circle formation with one player in center. Players move the ball around the circle but may not pass to players next to them. When the center player is able to touch ball, she switches places with the passer.
6. Leader facing a single line standing side-by-side. Use two balls, number one and the leader throw simultaneously; one throws to the leader and the leader throws to player number two. The next time the leader throws to player number three, then four, and so

1 2 3 4 5 6
LEADER

Figure 3

on. This demands that the leader be able to watch both balls at the same time.

7. Three players use two balls. Two players, each holding a ball, stand side by side facing the third person or leader. They throw alternately to the leader who returns the ball to the passer. Each time the players, standing side by side, receive the ball, they take one step sideward away from each other. They throw rapidly so that the leader must develop her peripheral vision because she is catching first from the right and then from the left.

LEADER

Figure 4

Moving Drills
1. Shuttle relay—At first attempt, players receive the ball standing still, pass and then run. Later they move to meet the ball.
2. Circle with leader (for very inexperienced groups)—All players run clockwise. Each player stops to receive the ball from the leader, passes back to her, and then runs on. Better passers are leaders. Circle changes directions frequently.

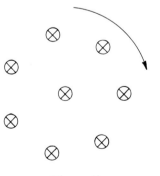

Figure 5

3. Two players pass back and forth while running the same direction. This is a good drill for inexperienced, intermediate and advanced players. Better players make longer passes and go at greater speeds.
4. Grapevine—Three players all facing the same direction move forward and pass the ball while weaving in and out. Player 1 makes the first pass to number 2 and cuts behind her; 2 passes to 3 and cuts behind 3, and 3 passes to 1 and cuts behind 1. Each player cuts close to the player to whom she passed and moves forward to receive the ball. (See Figure 6.)

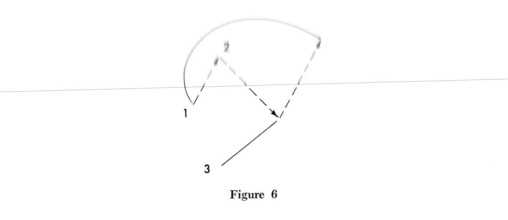

Figure 6

Shooting

Being able to shoot the ball into the basket is one of the most important offensive skills. It is much easier to motivate players to practice shooting skills than to practice many of the other offensive techniques. In shooting, however, players should be encouraged to practice good form rather than being allowed to aimlessly or haphazardly throw the ball at the basket. Inexperienced players should practice short shots to develop good form without the difficulty of straining to get the ball to the basket.

The problems of how much arch, how much spin, and how to aim the ball are not easily settled. When the ball drops from directly above the basket in a line of flight at a 90° angle with the rim of the basket, the full area of the basket is available to the ball. With a 9½-inch diameter ball and an 18-inch diameter basket, the ball can be 4½ inches from the center of the basket and still drop within the rim. If the ball approaches at an angle of 60° with the plane of the rim of the basket, only .87 of the inside area of the basket is available as a target. When the angle is reduced to 45°, a total of .71 of the area of the basket is open to the ball, and when the angle drops to 30°, the area drops to .50 of the inside diameter of the basket.[1]

With this information, it can be seen that a shot which does not hit the backboard has a greater chance for success if it has a high arch. There are, however, some drawbacks to shooting with a high arch. The ball travels a greater distance, and more strength is required of the shooter. In addition, because of greater momentum caused by the acceleration of gravity, the ball will rebound with more force if it strikes the rim. Mortimer therefore concluded that a ball which approaches the basket at an angle of 58° from a distance of 12 feet produces the greatest accuracy and that a 54° projection is most desirable for a 16 foot shot.[2]

Accuracy also involves the problem of backspin. It is desirable to impart backspin when shooting, especially with banked shots. Since the backspin makes the ball's fall more nearly vertical when rebounding from the backboard, it increases the possibility of the ball's dropping into the basket.

Finally the question of where to aim when shooting is controversial. Teachers frequently make charts showing the floor divided into sections.

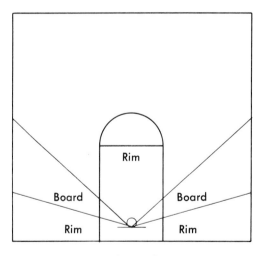

Figure 7

1. John W. Bunn, *Scientific Principles of Coaching* (Englewood Cliffs, N. J.: Prentice-Hall, Inc., 1955), p. 222.
2. Elizabeth Mortimer, "Basketball Shooting," *Research Quarterly of the American Association for Health, Physical Education, and Recreation,* May, 1951, p. 237.

They then suggest that players shooting from an area approximately 45° from the backboard aim at the backboard, and players shooting from the front and sides aim at the basket. Many coaches and teachers believe, however, that it is better for players to aim for the basket on all set shots and to bank the ball on lay-ups, hooks, and pivot shots. Teachers usually agree that when aiming for the basket the player should focus her eyes on the front rim and attempt to drop the ball over the rim.

It is difficult to determine a specific spot on the backboard at which players should aim because position on the floor, height of the arc, and the amount of ball spin affect the rebound. Players can, however, be taught that a ball without spin rebounds at an angle equal to that at which it strikes the board. Players should learn to shoot soft shots and to avoid forceful shots that hit the board or rim and carom off with little chance of dropping into the basket. The shooter also must be taught to develop fingertip control and a feel for the ball.

Lay-Up Shot

This shot is the most fundamental to the game, and it is the easiest way to score if the player can lose her opponent. The player starts the ball in two hands and then continues to reach with one hand so that the ball is "laid" against the backboard. The ball is lifted, not thrown. While the player's arm extension is the action that elevates the ball, the shot is released from the fingers. The player should be at a 45° angle with the backboard. When the ball is shot from the right it should have slight spin to the left as this will help the ball rebound toward the basket as it drops from the backboard.

It is desirable for the player to shoot with the right hand when shooting from the right side of the basket and with the left hand when shooting to the left of the basket. In this way the shooter uses her outside hand or the one away from a guarding player—it is much more difficult for the opponent to block such a shot. Shooting with the nonpreferred hand does not come naturally, however, and beginning players find it easier to develop the shot with the same arm from either side. If the player shoots with the right hand, she must take the last step with the left foot and bring the right knee up to gain elevation on the jump. The player should try for as much height as possible when executing the lay-up shot. The player should land on both feet with knees bent, ready to continue play. Although a beginning player needs to practice this movement slowly, she should be encouraged to improve her speed until she is able to run at full speed. Sometimes players coast on the last step instead of driving all the way. If a player is running to receive a pass, she should step left, catch the ball while in the air, step right, step left and shoot. If a player is moving straight toward the basket (down the center of the court), she should not bank the ball but drop it over the front rim.

Common Errors
1. Throwing the ball by using upper arm inward rotation rather than arm extension.
2. Pausing before the shot.
3. Traveling or taking off from the incorrect foot.
4. Shooting too far from the basket.

Coaching Points
1. Help players develop a soft touch. They must understand that the ball is lifted, not thrown. Have a player stand two or three feet from a wall and lift the ball to a spot on the wall so that it drops vertically. This is the movement which is used in the one hand push shot.
2. Practice footwork drills where players run without the ball, trying for a continuous takeoff.

Drills
1. Players practice the shot standing still under the basket.
2. Players practice the shot by stepping left and shooting, while working for more and more height.
3. Players take a dribble approach and shoot.
4. Players form a line and break for the basket to receive a pass and then shoot. With inexperienced players, teachers may find it better to use a permanent passer stationed at the free throw line. The person in this position should be skillful at passing.
5. Two lines facing the basket at a 45° angle to the backboard. Players should stay back until their turn, then break at full speed to shoot or rebound. Encourage good rebounding. In this drill, the ball should never touch the floor. Line at the right of the basket shoots and the other line rebounds and passes to the shooting line. Alternate shooting from the left line and then move the line so players break down the middle to shoot.

Underhand Lay-Up
The player's body movement is the same as for the orthodox lay-up shot. The player carries the ball toward the basket by an underhand movement, with the palm facing the ceiling.

Crossover Lay-Up

The player starts from in front and to one side of the basket. If the player starts from the left side, she moves across in front of the basket and shoots from the right side with the right hand. The player rotates her body to the left so that her shoulders face the basket. This is not a very difficult movement for the player who has already learned the lay-up, but it is much more difficult crossing from right to left unless the player shoots with the left hand.

Cross Under Lay-Up

If the player moving parallel to the end line is unable to shoot, she can continue under the basket, lean backward, and lift the ball against the backboard. If she is moving toward the left corner of the court, she shoots with the inside or right hand. She does not rotate the body on this shot, but leans backward with her face toward the ceiling and her eyes focused on the backboard. She carries the ball upward with her palm facing the ceiling and her thumb toward the backboard.

One Hand Push Shot

The one hand push shot can be used as a set shot or a moving shot. If the shot is performed while moving, the player's left foot is the

Cross Under Lay-Up

takeoff foot if she shoots with the right hand; this results in greater elevation. When the one hand push shot is used as a set shot, the player's right foot is forward. There is only slight weight transfer because most of the weight is forward on the right foot at the beginning of the shot. The player's knees are bent in preparation for the shot and extend as the ball is released. If necessary, her feet may leave the floor to provide added momentum.

Her arm movement follows the same pattern as the one used in the lay-up shot. She holds the ball in both hands in front of her chest, the left hand under the ball and the right hand behind it. She extends the right arm and flexes the hand as she releases the ball.

Common Errors
1. Lack of wrist flexion.
2. Failure to coordinate leg and arm extension when executing a set shot.

Coaching Points
1. Have player lift her arm up rather than pushing forward. Sometimes having player hold the follow-through helps to give awareness of arm movement.
2. Demonstrate how wrist action is restricted unless the arm is properly elevated. Having the player hold the follow-through of her hand allows her to see her hand position.

Chest Shot

This shot is used as either a short or long set shot. It is used most frequently for long outside shots. It is considered the best shot for distance shooting because more power is imparted to the ball by two hands than by one. The player holds the ball in the position for the chest pass and moves the arms the same way but she elevates her arms to give a higher arch to the ball. The player starts the ball at chest height and moves it upward. A player should avoid using a downward circular motion preceding the upward thrust because such movement gives the defensive player an advantage. This shot is diminishing in popularity as it is slow to execute.

Common Errors
1. Failure to get full arm extension.
2. Pushing more with one hand than the other.
3. Turning the elbows out away from the body.

Coaching Points
1. Get a complete follow-through with full arm extension. The hands rotate inwardly as the thumbs move forward giving a slight backspin to the ball. The hands end in a slight hyperextended position.
2. Keep the ball close to the chest with the hands at the side of the ball and the thumbs behind the ball.
3. Try to correct "elbows out" by concentrating on hand position. If the fingers point forward and the hands rotate inwardly, it will be very difficult to turn the elbows out.

Two Hand Overhead Shot

This shot is used most effectively by tall players. It is a good shot for a player when she receives a high pass under the basket or takes an offensive rebound. Her hands are at the sides and slightly under the ball, and the power comes from wrist action. The player holds the ball above her forehead rather than behind her head. She can deliver the shot with or without a jump.

This shot can be used very effectively as a set shot because it is difficult to guard. However, the shot requires strong wrists from any distance from the goal.

Common Errors
1. Player executes the shot by forward arm swing rather than wrist flexion.
2. Player is slow in executing shot and allows opponents to tie the ball.

Coaching Points
1. Have player keep the ball above the front part of the head and use strong wrist action.
2. Have player keep the thumbs under the ball.

Jump Shot

This shot, developed late in the history of basketball, has had a profound effect upon the game. It is very difficult to stop and can be executed from almost anywhere on the floor, except at great distances from the basket. The player holds the ball in both hands close to the body and brings the ball above her head into shooting position as she jumps. Her left hand rotates to the front and side of the ball, and her right hand is behind and under the ball. It could be said that the right hand shoots the ball out of the left hand. The player's left hand is in a position to protect the ball as it leaves her hands.

Jump Shot

Although the player's right elbow is bent at the beginning of the shot and extends in shooting, the main source of power for the shot comes from the wrist and fingers. The player must develop strong wrist action in order to be successful with this shot. The player's feet should be close together for the jump, and her movement should be straight up (for body balance). The shot is delivered at the top of the jump. The player's eyes should be focused on the basket. Beginning players will have trouble learning to coordinate the shot with the leg action. They should be encouraged to start at distances of five or six feet from the basket. The use of a lighter ball such as a volleyball or soccer ball might be helpful in the early stages of learning.

Common Errors
1. Failing to get the right hand into shooting position; the player uses both hands.
2. Player shoots with a flat trajectory rather than an arc.
3. Player does not coordinate shot with jump.

Coaching Points
1. Player must be taught to use strong wrist action of the right hand. This movement is very similar to that used in the one hand push shot. Player keeps the fingers of the right hand in spread position.
2. Urge players to stay close to basket until they develop some control of body movement.

Drills
Drill formations are not used very often to teach shooting. There are devices such as games and charts which will improve motivation, if this is needed. Players should be taught to get the shot off quickly rather than to take aim leisurely. Putting a premium on the number of baskets made in a certain amount of time will accomplish this. Players should also be taught to shoot with an opponent in front of them. Drills such as the one-on-one, page 10, will give practice in this.

Hook Shot
The hook shot usually is executed from a pivot position. While it can be used as a driving shot going down the side, it is rarely executed this way. The hook shot is extremely valuable because it is difficult to guard when the defensive player is faced with a one-on-one situation.

The player stands in the lane in side stride position with her back to the basket. She holds the ball in both hands in front of her chest. To shoot with the right hand, the player glides the left foot sideward and slightly backward as she begins to rotate to point the left shoulder toward the basket. She moves the ball to the right side with the right hand under the ball. As her left hand comes off the ball, it remains high to protect the shot. As her right leg crosses over in front of her body, she brings her right knee high. The player's eyes are focused on the board where she is aiming. She swings the right arm upward with the elbow straight and releases the ball from the

Hook Shot

fingertips. The shooter should avoid too much wrist action. If the ball is "wrist whipped," it will have a lower trajectory and too much force. As in the other shots, the player should shoot softly, using fingertip control.

Common Errors
1. Failing to get enough body rotation; the player moves away from the basket.
2. Holding the ball too long; the player flattens the arc.
3. Player uses too much wrist action.

Coaching Points
1. Emphasize a smooth flowing movement so that the body and arm actions are continuous and the player is moving for the rebound at the conclusion of the shot.
2. Have the player keep the ball high in preparation for the shot.
3. Emphasize handling the ball with a soft touch.

Drills

Since this shot is usually practiced from the pivot position, a definite progression can be established which would not apply to other shots.

1. Player stands at a 45° angle to the backboard, with shoulder of nonshooting side toward the basket. She practices the arm swing and the point of aim.
2. Player assumes a position 8 feet in front of the basket in the center of the lane with back to the basket. She glides the left foot to the side, pivots and shoots.
3. Same as 2 with a defensive player standing between shooter and basket. Guard does not move.
4. Same as 3 with a defensive player actively guarding.
5. Same as 3 except that the shooter receives the ball from a teammate.
6. Same as 5 except that the teammate feeds the shooter as the shooter moves across the lane. Try this first with no defensive player and then later add one.

Two Hand Underhand (free throw shot)

Since any shot may be used from the free throw line, many teachers advocate that the player use the shot that seems easiest for her. If a player uses the one hand push or the chest shot, she will be practicing techniques which will be used at other times during a game. But since the free throw attempt is an unguarded shot, the two hand underhand throw is an appropriate shot for this attempt, and it is one of the easier movements for beginners.

The player should stand in a comfortable side stride position directly in front of the basket and within an inch of the free throw line. Some players prefer to have one foot slightly behind the other. The player holds the ball in the fingers with the hands at the sides of the ball. The player's weight is on the balls of her feet. As the player lowers the ball she bends the knees, keeping the back fairly erect. She straightens her legs as her arms swing upward. The shooter should focus on the front rim of the basket and attempt to drop the ball over the front rim. The ball should have a slight backspin.

Common Errors

1. Player bends too far forward from the hips.

2. Poor arc. If the player releases the ball too soon, the arc will be too flat; if she releases too late, the arc will be too high and the ball may not reach the basket.

Coaching Points
1. Shooter should relax before attempting shot. Teaching the shooter to bounce the ball or take a deep breath may help the shooter to relax.
2. Try to instill confidence in players.
3. Teach the players to be consistent in stance, grip, and shot.

Dribble

The main use of the dribble is to cover distance. It is also used to consume time as a teammate gets into position or to kill time while controlling the ball in the last minutes of a game. Many beginning

Dribble

players overuse the dribble. It is a slow method of advancing the ball because the ball can be passed much faster than it can be dribbled.

The dribbler bends the knees and bends slightly at the hips while keeping the head up with the eyes forward rather than on the ball. She contacts the ball with the cushions of the thumbs and fingers but not the palm. The dribbler's fingers are slightly spread, and she bounces the ball with a pumping action of her hand, wrist, and arm. She should keep the ball low for better control, but she may dribble high if there are no opponents near. Greater speed and distance result from a high dribble. If a player is driving to her right around an opponent, she should dribble with the right hand, and if she moves to her left she should use the left hand. By using the outside hand to control the dribble, she puts the ball farther from the opponent and imposes her body as a screen for the ball. The nondribbling arm should be carried high to make a more effective screen and keep the opponent farther from the ball. All players should be encouraged to learn to dribble skillfully with either hand.

Common Errors
1. Player slaps at the ball with the palm.
2. Player uses a high vertical bounce.
3. Player travels by lifting the pivot foot before releasing the ball.
4. Player watches the ball.
5. Player dribbles with the ball on the side instead of in front of the body.

Coaching Points
1. Teach the player to keep the wrist and fingers flexible.
2. Try to have the player control the ball with a low bounce.
3. Have the player keep the ball well ahead of the body.
4. Have the player adjust the angle of the ball to her speed.

Drills
1. Single file—First girl dribbles continuously to the end of the gym and back. She dribbles with the right hand one direction and with the left for the other. She then goes to the end of the line.
2. Same as 1 with a defensive player opposing the dribbler. Allow 25 to 30 feet between the lines.
3. Shuttle formation—dribbler limited to three bounces.
4. Single file—Players or chairs are placed in a straight line with 10 feet separating them. Dribbler weaves in and out between these players or obstacles, using the outside hand.

Pivots

The pivot and the reverse turn provide ways of evading an opponent. They might be used by an offensive player who may or may not have the ball. The pivot can also be used by a defensive player as when blocking out an opponent on a rebound.

The reverse turn is usually classified as a pivot. Since it is easy to understand and used in almost all sports the reverse turn is sometimes overlooked in basketball instruction. Yet when done skillfully at great speed, it requires good body balance and agility. In coming to a stop in a forward stride position, the weight should be kept low. The reverse is made on the balls of the feet while they are in contact with the floor. If the right foot is forward, the turn would be to the left. The player should get a good push from the forward foot to make the reverse as quickly as possible. The reverse turn can be incorporated into warm-up drills or drills for conditioning.

In addition to the reverse turn there are two types of pivots, the front and the rear. The front of the body leads when a player executes a front pivot, and the rear of the body leads when a player does a rear pivot. If a player lifts the left foot and steps across in front of her right, she thus has executed a front pivot; but if she lifts her left foot and carries it behind her right foot, she has done a rear pivot.

When a player with the ball is facing an opponent and wants to pivot and drive to her right around the left side of the opponent, she must use her right foot as the pivot foot. This is true for both the front and rear pivot. When a player pivots to her right, she will use the right foot as a pivot foot, and when she pivots to her left, she will use the left foot.

Since the main objective of the pivot is to evade an opponent, the pivot must draw a defensive player off balance. When executing a pivot, the player should keep her weight low by bending her knees. The heel of the pivot foot comes off the floor and the weight is on the ball of the foot. If the player wishes to pivot and dribble, she must push with the pivot foot in order to get the jump on the defensive player. Using a preliminary feint will aid in this.

Common Errors
1. Player's weight is carried too high for good body balance.
2. Player's movement is slow and jerky.
3. Player takes a very small step and does not evade guard.

Coaching Points
1. Player must keep the knees bent.

2. Player must keep the ball close to her body.
3. Player must always protect the ball from the opponent.

Drills

1. Scattered formation—each player practices footwork.
2. Players work in pairs without using balls. One player works on pivots against the other player who plays defensively.
3. Same as 2 but with ball, no dribbling permitted. The defensive player tries to tie the ball. A second defensive player can be added for more advanced players.
4. Rear pivot can be learned in a circle formation. Ball is passed around the circle; players pivot to outside of circle. A defensive player can be used in the center of the circle.
5. Shuttle formation. Players pivot, dribble, and pass.
6. Same as 5 except players dribble first and then pivot and pass.

Cut

A cut is a sudden movement into a space, made in an attempt to lose a defensive player. It is done by an offensive player who does not have the ball. The word "break" is synonymous with "cut." The cut can be in any direction but is usually made toward the basket. If the player breaks between the ball and the defensive player, it is an inside cut; if the player breaks behind the defensive player, it is

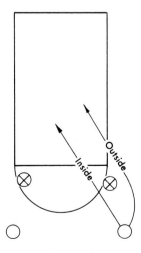

Figure 8

an outside cut. An outside cut to the basket is sometimes called a back door play.

If the player does an inside cut, she places herself between her opponent and the ball and has a clear passing lane to receive the ball. If she gets ahead of the defensive player on an outside cut, she has also gained a passing lane. If the defensive player stays with the offensive player on an outside cut, the offensive player is not free for a pass. A player must develop a sense of timing in order to make her break coincide with a teammate's pass. She must be deceptive in her movements so that the defensive player cannot anticipate her moves.

Common Errors
1. Player fails to create a space and has no area in which to cut.
2. Player fails to see a space and move into it.
3. Player fails to coordinate move with teammates' play.

Coaching Points
Beginning players do not think about creating a space or do not see it if it is there. It takes an experienced player and a patient coach or teacher to produce a game of "thinking" basketball. The concept of pulling out a guard and cutting is fundamental to offensive play, and plays such as the give-and-go and the screen-and-roll are based on the principle of cutting. Beginning players should be stopped in game play and shown an opportunity for a cut when they fail to take advantage of it.

Drills
1. Two-on-one. Start this practice with the defensive player assigned to one of the offensive players and have the defensive player remain stationary for the first few trials.

   If O_1 becomes the passer and O_2 the cutter, O_1 is practicing passing to a breaking player while avoiding passing into the defensive player directly in front of her. After practicing this simple drill, the players will be ready for a two-on-one in which the defensive player plays the ball and takes either opponent.

2. Cutting off the post. The post or pivot player assumes a position at the free throw line with her back to the basket. Two single files of players face the post. The first one in each line crosses in front of the post and is ready for a hand off. The player passing the ball makes the first cut.

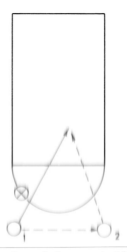

Figure 9. O_1 passes to O_2 and does an inside cut for a return pass. O_1 should practice both inside and outside cuts. (This is the give-and-go.)

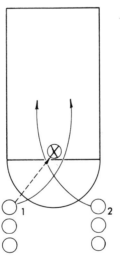

Figure 10. O_1 passes to the post and breaks to her own right, O_2 cuts to her own left so that the two players crisscross in front of the post.

Timing is important because the players move around the post almost simultaneously. They cut close to the pivot player because in a game this action might eliminate the defensive player from the play. The pivot passes to either one of the cutting players who attempts a lay-up. After the players have finished their turn, they go to the end of the opposite line.

Feint

A feint is a pretense to deceive the opponent and make her move. Feints, or fakes as they are sometimes called, can be made with the ball or with the head, eyes, shoulders or feet. Any feint is followed by a quick movement in a different direction. The feint is a good offensive maneuver for a player with or without the ball. A player who develops this skill to a high degree seems to fake by habit and without thinking, making it appear that this is a natural ability rather than an acquired one. When inexperienced players overfake, however, they slow the game and waste energy. A player must remember that it is not practical to feint unless her opponent is close enough to be outmaneuvered. The fake must be quick and deft enough to force the defensive player to defend against it. Some of the common feints with the ball are:

1. Fake a shot, and pass.
2. Fake a shot, and then drive.
3. Fake a shot, and attempt a delayed shot.
4. Fake a drive, and then shoot.
5. Fake a drive, and drive to the opposite side; make use of the cross-over step, one form of the front pivot.
6. Fake a drive to one side and then go to that same side; make use of the rocker motion when executing this play. The player starts in side stride position and steps forward on the right foot, faking a drive to her right. She then brings the right foot back behind her left foot, shifting the weight to the right foot. If her opponent retreated with the left foot and then brought the left foot forward, the offensive player starts the forward rocker motion again, only this time she goes. She moves the right foot forward, shifting the weight to the forward foot. As she lifts the right foot to start backward in order to get the defensive player to shift her weight forward, she pushes with the left foot and starts the drive.

When a player does not have the ball, she uses all of the same body fakes in order to lose a defensive player. She may fake an outside cut by running hard to her right, planting the right foot and using a reverse turn, pushing off hard with the right foot and cutting to the left inside her guard. Being able to make fast stops and starts is part of getting free from a defensive player.

Common Errors
1. Player carries weight too high when faking with the feet.
2. Player lacks deception.

Coaching Points
1. Have player keep knees well bent and push hard against the floor for a fast start.
2. Insist that the player fake only when the defensive player is within four or five feet. If the defensive player is farther away, she can be fooled but may recover in time.

Drills
1. Players work on reverse turn in forward-backward position by running forward and reversing direction at the sound of the whistle.
2. Same drill except players run making a large lap around the gymnasium, making a 90° turn at each corner. With small numbers of players, half of the basketball court may be used. In addition to making the right angle turn at the corners, the players reverse direction at the whistle. A double blast on the whistle can be used for a full stop. Players should practice both stride stops and jump stops.
3. Drills 2 and 5 described under Footwork in Chapter 2, pages 9 and 10. When using drill number 5 (one-on-one), the offensive player could be told that she had to use a minimum of three fakes before a shot may be attempted.

Screen

A screen is an offensive technique used to block the desired movement of an opponent. In one of the simplest forms of the screen a player without the ball stands between a teammate and the basket to allow the teammate an unguarded shot. (See Figures 12 and 13.)

A player may assume any position when screening, but she may not use personal contact to block an opponent. She should avoid the position of both arms extended sideward since blocking will be called if body contact occurs as the defensive player attempts to move around the screen. The players should learn the concept of screening with the body rather than the arms, as beginners sometimes tend to do.

The use of the side screen is a little more difficult and players should practice the more elementary form of the screen before attempting the side or lateral screen. When setting a screen at the side of

Good Screening Position

a defensive player in an attempt to free a teammate for a drive to that side, the player must choose the right angle for the screen. The screen should be made so that it is difficult for the defensive player to slip in front of it or drift behind it. The player making the screen should face the defensive player and be within six to eight inches of her. She should have a fairly wide stance so that one foot is well ahead of the opponent and the other behind her. The screener should bend at the knees and hips and create a large obstruction to the opponent.

GUARD   GUARD   SCREEN

Correct angle   **Figure 11**   Incorrect angle
Screen for drive to the right

Successful screening requires an acute sense of timing by the two offensive players. The player with the ball cannot move until the screen is set as she may cause her teammate to foul. If the dribbler moves too soon the defensive player usually will be able to beat the screen. When she drives past the screening teammate she should go as close to the shoulder of her teammate as possible. This play usually results in the dribbler evading the defensive player as the opponent finds herself picked off in the play. This type of screen is sometimes referred to as a pick.

Common Errors
1. Teammates do not coordinate movements.
2. Player making the screen gets a poor angle on the defensive player who is able to slip around the screen.

Coaching Points
1. Players must work on this play over and over. No two people screen quite the same way and players must learn to work together.
2. Player making the screen must get close to the defensive player and occupy space in order to be successful in blocking the defensive player out of the play.

Drills
1. Two-on-two. Player with the ball passes to teammate and cuts behind her for a return pass and a set shot.

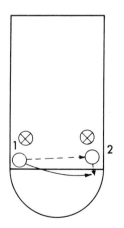

Figure 12. O_1 passes to O_2 and cuts behind her for a set shot. O_2 does a rear pivot to the right and makes a stationary screen.

This is about the simplest form of the screen. The same play could be done at the side as shown in Figure 13.

2. The drill shown in Figure 14 is a little more difficult as the screener must move into position.

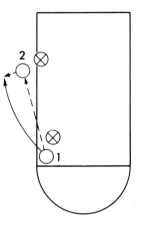

Figure 13. O_1 passes to O_2 and breaks behind her for a return pass. O_2 does a rear pivot to the left and screens for O_1 as she attempts a set shot.

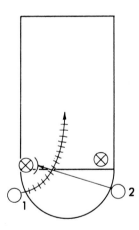

Figure 14. O_1 has the ball. O_2 moves to screen and O_1 drives behind her and goes for a lay-up. This works better if the ball starts with O_2 and she starts to move across with a dribble and then moves into screening position. This is called an inside screen. If the screen were on the other side of the defensive player, that is, between the defensive player and the sideline, it would be called an outside screen.

Roll

The roll is an offensive maneuver designed to evade an opponent. It is a form of the rear pivot and can be used by a dribbler but is more often used by a player without the ball. If a player is running and comes to a stride stop with the right foot forward, she wheels or rolls to her right by doing a rear pivot to her right and continues moving. The roll is often combined with a screen for the purpose of getting an inside position on a defensive player.

Common Errors
1. Player fails to get a good angle on a screen preceding the roll.
2. Player lacks knee bend to insure good push off.

Coaching Points
1. Insist player pause slightly with the screen and then continue moving with the roll.
2. Have player turn so that her back is to the defensive player.
3. The screening player should be coached "to split the defense," that is, to roll between the two defensive players. (See Figure 16.)

Drills
1. Scattered formation. Everyone tries footwork pattern.

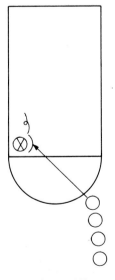

Figure 15

2. One-on-one using a stationary defensive player. From a single file, a player moves to screen the defensive player and rolls to a back-to-back position and goes to end of line. (See Figure 15.)
3. Same as drill Number 2 for the screen. (See Figure 16.)

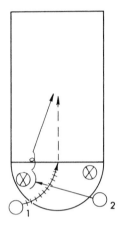

Figure 16. O_2 moves to screen, rolls to an inside position on the defensive player and receives a pass from O_1 who started to dribble around the screen.

REFERENCES

1. Anderson, Forrest. *Basketball Techniques Illustrated.* New York: A. S. Barnes and Co., 1952.
2. Auerbach, Arnold. *Basketball for the Player, the Fan and the Coach.* New York: Pocket Books, Inc., 1952.
3. Broer, Marion. *Efficiency of Human Movement.* Philadelphia: W. B. Saunders Co., 1966.
4. Bunn, John W. *Scientific Principles of Coaching.* Englewood Cliffs, N. J.: Prentice-Hall, Inc., 1955.
5. Healy, William. *High School Basketball, Coaching, Managing, Administering.* Danville, Ill.: The Interstate Printers and Publishers, Inc., 1962.
6. Lawrence, Helen, and Fox, Grace. *Basketball for Girls and Women.* New York: McGraw-Hill Book Co., Inc., 1954.
7. McGuire, Frank. *Offensive Basketball.* Englewood Cliffs, N. J.: Prentice-Hall, Inc., 1958.
8. Meyer, Margaret, and Schwarz, Marguerite. *Team Sports for Girls and Women.* Philadelphia: W. B. Saunders Co., 1965.
9. Miller, Donna Mae, and Ley, Katherine. *Individual and Team Sports for Women.* Englewood Cliffs, N. J.: Prentice-Hall, Inc., 1955.
10. Miller, Kenneth D., and Horky, Rita Jean. *Modern Basketball for Women.* Columbus. Ohio: Charles E. Merrill Co., 1970.

11. Mortimer, Elizabeth. "Basketball Shooting." *Research Quarterly of the American Association for Health, Physical Education, and Recreation,* May, 1951.

12. Mullaney, David. "Free Throw Technique." *Athletic Journal,* November, 1957.

13. Neal, Patsy. *Basketball Techniques for Women.* New York: Ronald Press Co., 1966.

14. Newell, Pete, and Benington, John. *Basketball Methods.* New York: Ronald Press Co., 1962.

15. Redin, Harley. *The Queens Fly High.* Plainview, Texas: Plainview Herald, 1958.

16. Teague, Bertha Frank. *Basketball for Girls.* New York: Ronald Press Co., 1962.

Systems of Defensive Play

Player-To-Player

In the player-to-player or man-to-man defense, one defensive player is assigned to one offensive player, and each defensive player has the sole responsibility for her individual opponent. Thus, in theory, every offensive player is covered all the time so baskets should be scored very rarely and only as the result of phenomenal shooting.

In practice, the player-to-player defense often works somewhat differently. The player-to-player defense will not work if the offensive player is able to outmaneuver her opponent. This system of defense becomes a series of individual struggles or contests—two players of opposing teams each trying to outwit or outmaneuver the other.

In addition to a series of one-in-one contests, the offense often tries to combine movements so the defensive player is faced not only with guarding her specific opponent but also with combating a screening opponent as well. Because of this, the defensive players sometimes find it necessary to switch their guarding assignments. But since switching by the defensive players should be done only in emergency situations, the difficult part of learning a player-to-player defense becomes learning when to switch. While a defense that never uses the switch might be effective against beginning players who are unfamiliar with a screen, it would allow an effective offense many unguarded shots. In addition the decision to switch must be made instantly, and both defensive players must react immediately. Inexperienced players using a switch may find that they have two players guarding one opponent while another opponent is slipping the ball in the basket unguarded.

A thinking team which realizes that the opposition is using a switching player-to-player defense will force switches that cause a mismatch. If the offensive team is able to cause a definite mismatch in height or speed, it will give the ball to the player who has an inadequate defensive player and hope that the offensive player will be able to score. In this situation, the defensive team may find the wisest plan is to eliminate switching.

The plan of an effective switch must be practiced and discussed until all the players are thoroughly familiar with it. A few principles should be established.

1. Defensive players do not switch when opponents are beyond the head of the circle.
2. A defensive player should slide through the space between a teammate and her opponent rather than move around another offensive player. (See Figure 17.)

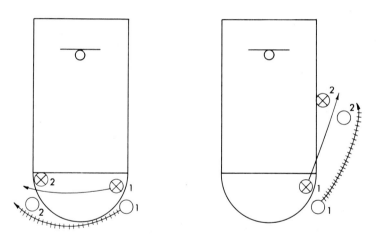

Figure 17. X_1 slides between X_2 and O_2. As X_1 slides through the opening, X_2 should back up a little to be sure that X_1 has room. X_2 may help by pushing X_1 through. X_2 would then resume her normal guarding position.

3. Defensive players should anticipate screens and try to avoid them by moving behind or in front of the screener. If possible, the defensive player should never let the opponent gain a screening position. (See Figure 18.)

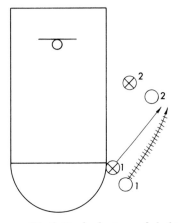

Figure 18. In Figure 17 if O_1 had stopped behind O_2, she would have had a shot. By aggressive play, X_1 could anticipate this move and prevent it by sliding in front of the screen.

4. When a successful screen is made, the defensive player who moves to the ball should call the switch because she has a better view of the play. Players should switch on a vocal signal only. (See Figure 19.)
5. Players do not switch on obvious mismatches.
6. Defensive players should talk to their teammates. Communicating information such as the location of the offensive players, impend-

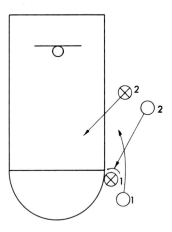

Figure 19. O_1 has the ball and O_2 moves into screening position. O_1 starts the drive for the basket. If X_1 can break out of O_2's screen, she will stay on her own opponent. X_2 is in position to take either O_1 or O_2. X_2 calls the switch.

ing screens, and the need for assistance helps build coordinated team play.

A team using the player-to-player defense must be alert to the threat of the pivot player. The player assigned to guard the pivot usually plays to the side or in front of the pivot in order to prevent her from receiving the ball. This is not true if the pivot player plays out as far as the free throw line in high post position. The other defensive players must assist the pivot guard in blocking the passing lanes to the pivot. This is best accomplished by having the front defensive player on the weak side sink toward the basket. (See Figure 20.)

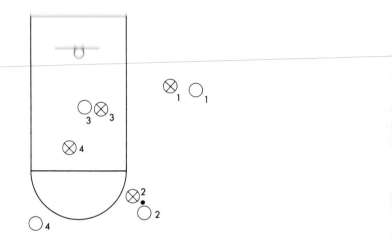

Figure 20. X_4 has dropped back from her opponent to help block a pass to the pivot.

The player guarding the pivot has a difficult assignment. Even though she can expect help from her teammates, she has this primary responsibility. The pivot plays in the best scoring area and usually is a tall player. She is an atypical player because she rarely faces the basket. If the pivot is adept at the hook shot, there is no way the pivot guard can stop her from the conventional guarding position. Because she plays in such a good scoring area and because an experienced pivot is almost impossible to stop, the defensive team must defend against a pass to the pivot player. This means the entire team, especially the pivot guard, must concentrate on never allowing the ball to be passed to this player while she remains in the pivot position.

The pivot guard should abandon the conventional defensive position between the opponent and the basket and move out to the side or in front of the pivot player. If the pivot assumes a very deep position (only one or two feet in front of the basket), the defensive player should play in front of her, between the pivot and the ball. The most common pattern of movement a pivot player follows is moving back and forth through the lane trying to get in position for a pass. If the pivot uses this pattern, the guard should take her position between the pivot and the ball and force the pivot away from the desired path. The guard should never let the pivot cut in front of her unless the pivot moves into high post position in the area of the free throw line. When the pivot guard forces her opponent to cut behind her, she should keep her hands high and block the passing lanes to the pivot.

When the pivot becomes stationary, the guard should play beside her with an outstretched arm ready to block the pass. The defensive player should be on the ball side of the pivot with her feet in a forward stride position. When the guard is defending from her right, the right foot is forward ahead of her opponent with the right arm reaching to block the ball. When guarding from the left, the foot and hand positions are reversed. The hand that is outstretched in front of the pivot should be facing the ball as this is the best position from which to make deflections. The defensive player must keep moving and always anticipate moves by the opponent because a motionless

Guarding the Pivot

guard is much easier to outmaneuver than is one who is constantly changing position. The guard must be alert for a lob pass which goes over her head to the pivot who is breaking for the basket.

The same principle of not allowing the pivot to receive the ball in a desirable position applies to other players. This is difficult for inexperienced players because of their lack of judgment and concentration. However, as players gain experience in techniques of guarding and understanding of defensive play, they can appreciate the importance of defending a player before she receives the ball. Offensive players have become so skillful with the ball that it is very difficult to prevent a good shot if the player receives the ball in an advantageous position.

When guarding a strong side forward in the corner position, the defensive player should move high to the side of the forward with the inside hand in front of the opponent to discourage a pass. If the forward moves toward the ball and then reverses in an outside cut, the defensive player should turn inside or toward the ball and play the interception.

Defensive players should work at improving their peripheral vision so that the opponent and the ball are kept in sight. They should keep moving and anticipating. A defensive player should try to harass and outwit her opponent, thus taking the initiative away from the offensive player. The offensive player should be prevented from receiving passes while cutting toward the basket as she will be much less dangerous if she receives the ball moving away from the basket.

The defensive team must be alert to the possibility of an opponent's driving around her guard and having a clear path to the goal. The other defensive players should help in a situation such as this, even to the point of leaving their individual opponents. The defensive players cannot afford to give unguarded easy shots to the opposition, and they must be prepared to cover for a teammate.

In Figure 20, if O_2 drives past X_2 and is moving for a lay-up, X_1 or X_3 must move to stop her drive. X_1 would be the better of the two because that would leave O_1 open and force a pass away from the basket. If O_3 is left unguarded, she would have an easy shot.

Defensive players should be alert for an opportunity to double team one opponent. To double team or two time, two defensive players converge on one opponent and try either to tie the ball or to force her into making a bad pass. The defensive player assisting in a double team must also remain aware of her own opponent. She can only aid her teammate (in a double team) if her assigned opponent is

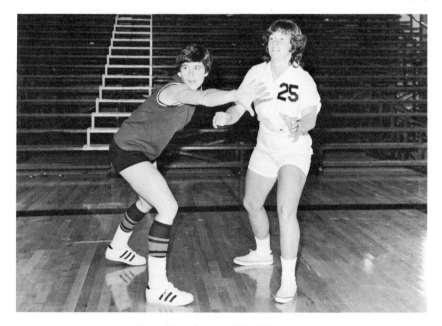

Guarding Strong Side Forward

Guarding Strong Side Forward

nearby. And, in case of a pass, she would be able to shift back immediately to her own player.

The player-to-player defense varies considerably in how tightly or loosely the players guard their opponents. This depends, in part, on the skill of the defensive players, on the ability of the opponents, and on the style of attack. If the opponents have good outside shooting, the defensive players will have to play a tight defensive game. If the outside shooting is not much of a threat, however, the defense can play back and concentrate more on stopping drives and collapsing on the pivot. If the offensive players are not too adept at ball handling, a tight defensive game could result in many interceptions.

Advantages of player-to-player defense over a zone type defense include:

1. The defense provides a more complete court coverage. It guards against long shots.
2. It is more effective against a stall.
3. It reinforces players' awareness of good individual defensive fundamentals.
4. The defensive players can be matched to opponents of same size, speed, or ability.
5. It allows a player to study one opponent well. This makes it possible to learn the strengths, weaknesses, and habits of this player more readily than if she were switching to several opponents.
6. The defense is suitable for more situations. It is equally usable whether a team is ahead or behind, while the zone defense must be discarded late in the game if the team is losing.

Zone Defense

All zones are based on the theory that each defensive player, rather than following an individual opponent, assumes a position in relation to the position of the ball. If the ball is always guarded, the opponents find it is very difficult to score. The defensive players concentrate their efforts in the area nearest the basket and force the opponents to pass the ball around the zone, or high over it, but never through it. In this system, there is always one person playing point for the defense, guarding the opponent with the ball. The other defensive players assume their positions behind the point and block all the possible angles of the ball's progress toward the basket. Players using a zone defense should always face the ball, keep their arms up, and use their feet and bodies to occupy space, thereby helping block the opponent's passing lanes.

The positioning of the body is very important when playing zone defense. Players should adopt the concept that the facing of the ball means the toes face the ball and the palms of the hands are open to the ball. The defensive players should present a large obstruction to thwart the opponents. Inexperienced players may have the head facing the ball but the body is slightly turned, thereby reducing the body surface exposed to the opponent and producing a smaller obstruction.

The players should be careful not to overextend the zone, thereby making penetration by the opponents less difficult. No system of zone defense will be able to give complete court coverage. As players become more skillful they will be able to cover a greater area of the court. It is wise for inexperienced or slow moving players to use a smaller tighter zone than to spread so far that the zone becomes ineffective.

The main advantage of using a zone defense is the concentration of the defense in the best scoring area, thereby allowing fewer short shots. If a team elects to move out to stop the outside shots, it has to give space on the inside. This increases the threat of a pivot player. If the opponents pass the ball to a pivot in low post position, the defense should converge on the ball and double team or triple team the pivot player.

Although the players using a zone should take their positions according to the position of the ball, they should also learn to make adjustments according to the positions of the other offensive players. Such judgment comes with experience. Beginning players learn more easily if they think only about blocking the angles of the possible passes, but an experienced defensive player will make an adjustment to compensate for change in floor position of an opponent who does not have the ball. In Figure 21, player X_5 could move toward X_2 to decrease the opening into which O_4 is trying to move. (See Figure 22.)

All defensive players should be coached to call movements of the opponents. X_5 should call "coming through" or "in the lane" as O_4 starts her movement. This alerts the front defensive players as to what is happening behind them. The use of the voice is very important for defensive play.

There are many styles of zone defense with the identification or name coming from the original defensive position. Thus, a 2-3 means two players in the front line of defense with three teammates behind them in a second line. However, as the ball is moved around the

Converging on the Pivot

court, the defensive alignment changes until one zone resembles another. A zone defense must function as a unit and players must learn positioning in relation to the situation. Therefore, a player should not think of maintaining a position in her zone of the left front area as she may be forced into the left deep area or the right front area. She takes her position according to the movement of the ball, and also the position of her teammates and opponents. This requires intelligent play on the part of defensive players. Some players seem to have instinctive game sense but for the majority many hours of practice are required.

If a zone defense is to be effective, the players must be committed to aggressive play. There is a temptation to relax a little and to have less "hustle" when players know that teammates are ready to cover for a mistake. A slow moving zone can be easily outmaneuvered by good passing.

The advantages of a zone defense over the player-to-player include:

1. Fewer short shots are allowed, since the defense is concentrated in the best scoring area.
2. It is more effective against a cutting offense.
3. It is more effective against a rolling screen offense.
4. Defensive players are in better rebounding positions.

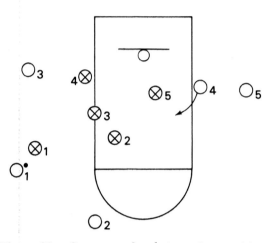

Figure 21. O_4 starts a break into pivot position.

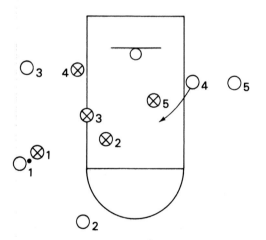

Figure 22. Notice the slight change of position of X_5 as she reduces the space for O_4.

5. Players commit fewer fouls because they play the ball rather than an opponent.
6. Players intercept more passes because they play the ball.
7. Players expend less energy.
8. A tall player not well qualified in individual defensive techniques can be used to greater advantage.
9. It provides good positioning for the start of a fast break.

Five of the more common zones will be presented. The diagrams indicate the approximate positions of the defensive players. However, these positions are subject to change depending on the individual abilities of the players and the positioning and abilities of the opponents.

TWO-THREE ZONE

This defense with two players out and three in was one of the earliest zones.

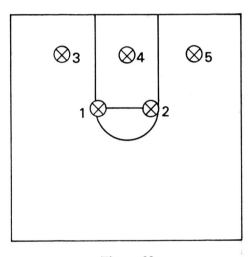

Figure 23

Advantages:

1. Excellent rebound positioning.
2. Good defense against corners.
3. Strong against low pivot play.
4. Strong defense in basket area.
5. Complements fast break attack.

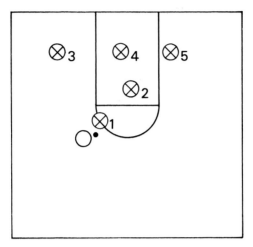

Figure 24

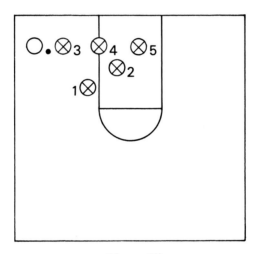

Figure 25

Weaknesses:
1. Weak against good outside shooting.
2. Weak in the high post area.

TWO-ONE-TWO ZONE

This zone developed from the two-three position, and was an attempt to better defend the high post position and the top of the circle. The best rebounder usually plays in the X_3 position.

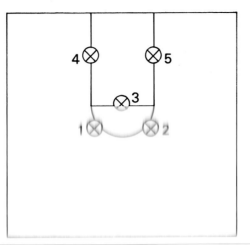

Figure 26

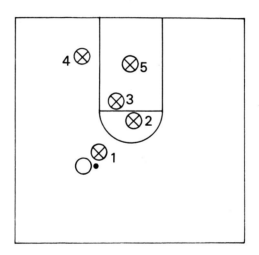

Figure 27

Advantages:

1. Good rebound positioning.
2. Good defense of vulnerable foul line area.
3. Strong defense in basket area.
4. Complements fast break attack.

Weaknesses:

1. Vulnerable to good baseline shots and moves.
2. Weak in corners.
3. Difficult to cover good outside shooting.

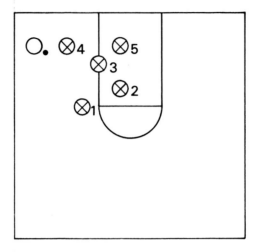

Figure 28

THREE-TWO ZONE

This is one of the older types of zones. The best personnel would be quick reacting hustling front line players with big strong deep players. With the development of the jump shot this defense is not used very extensively.

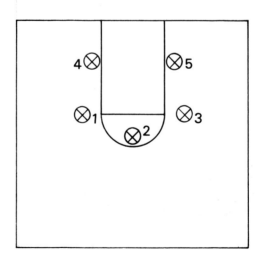

Figure 29

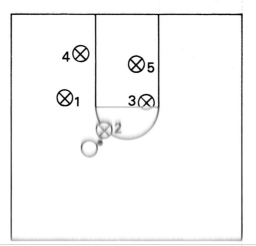

Figure 30

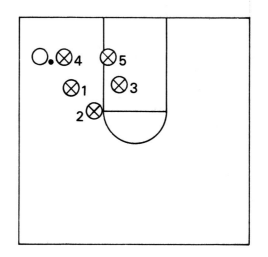

Figure 31

Advantages:

1. Strong against outside shooting.
2. Good fast break possibilities.
3. Strong against poor ball handling guards.
4. Discourages good drivers in front.

Weaknesses:

1. Very weak once front line is penetrated.
2. Poor rebound positioning.

3. Weak in corners.

4. Vulnerable to good baseline shots and moves.

ONE-THREE-ONE ZONE

This defense was developed to strengthen the foul line area. The biggest player would play the X_3 position and a fast player should be given the X_5 position as she will have to cover both corners.

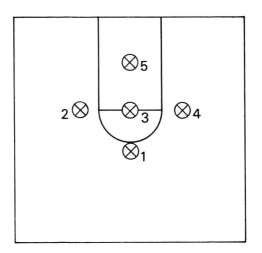

Figure 32

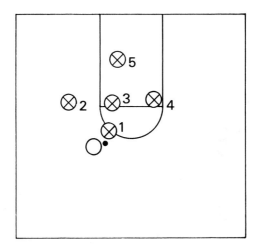

Figure 33

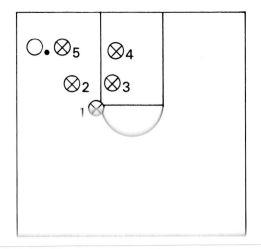

Figure 34

Advantages:

1. Strong in the foul line area.
2. Minimizes post attack.
3. Requires the offense to make considerable adjustment to their normal zone patterns.

Weaknesses:

1. Poor rebound positioning.
2. Difficult to run the fast break from this alignment.
3. Very vulnerable to good corner shooting.
4. Vulnerable to short jump shots along the baseline.

ONE-TWO-TWO

This is one of the more recent types of zones to be used and calls for a very agile player to play the X_1 position.

Advantages:

1. Discourages guards from driving.
2. Good sneak away opportunities for X_1.
3. Strong against low post.
4. Strong against good outside shooting.

Weaknesses:

1. Weak in corners.
2. Vulnerable to good baseline shots and moves.
3. Somewhat weak in rebounding.

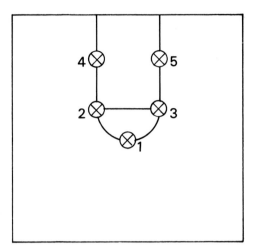

Figure 35

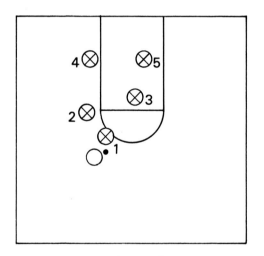

Figure 36

FOUR PLAYER ZONE
(With the Fifth Player Guarding
Player-to-Player)

Some teams have an offense built around one high scoring player. In such a situation, it may be best to assign a good defensive player to cover the shooter and have the other four defensive players use

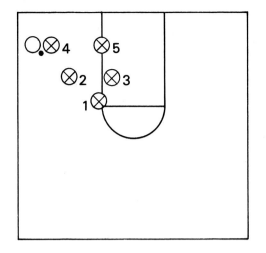

Figure 37

a zone. This arrangement is most effective if the high scorer plays from the head of the circle or in the corner. If the outstanding scorer is the pivot a tight zone might be the best defense.

The defensive player assigned to the shooter should attempt to prevent her opponent from receiving the ball. This means a change from her usual style of play. If the shooter fakes to the basket, the defensive player should be instructed not to follow the fake. The offensive player is using a fake in order to have maneuvering room to get the ball. A cut to the basket is not dangerous because of the zone.

More than one player should be able to undertake the defensive assignment of guarding the high scoring opponent. This type of play is hard work and the player may tire. She may find herself in foul trouble because of the aggressive style of play.

This type of defense is sometimes called a combination defense as both zone and player to player are used. It is also referred to as a zone with a chaser. The four player zone can be a two-two or box, or it can be a one-two-one or diamond.

Press

The press has gained in popularity in recent years. Although it has long been used, the press was considered to be a desperation defense usually reserved until late in the game. With a greater development of this defense some teams have adopted it as their standard style of play. In the early use of the press most teams employed a player-to-player style of play, but the greater development in modern basketball has led to many varieties of both zone and player-to-player.

The basic theory of the press is to put pressure on the offensive team and force it into mistakes in order to cause interceptions, loose balls, violations, and in general to disrupt the planned offensive game. The defensive team hopes to surprise and confuse its opponents.

One of the most common times to use the press is late in the game when behind. Other situations in which the press might be advantageous include: against poor ball handling teams, teams in poor condition, inexperienced teams, clubs with poor dribbling guards, slow teams and tense, nervous opponents. The press is a good technique for speeding up the tempo of the game and can be used effectively against a ball control type of offense. If a team has players with good speed but not a lot of height, it may find the press to be the most effective style of defense.

There are, however, inherent weaknesses in the press. Because the defense is spread into a wide area, it is vulnerable to a sudden break for the basket and a resulting short shot. Once the offensive team members have penetrated the press, they will have much more space from which to maneuver and to shoot even if they are not able to go for the short shot. In addition fouls may be more frequent with this type of defense because it requires aggressive play. Players must be in excellent condition to use this more complete defensive court coverage.

The players must understand that using the press is a gamble. It can prove to be a poor gamble if the players do not understand its weaknesses and do not use good judgment in different situations. If an unfavorable situation arises, the defense should know how to withdraw to a more compact, less vulnerable formation.

Either the player-to-player or zone press may be used on the full court, three-quarter court, or the half court. Some basic rules of the press include:

1. The defensive team is not trying to grab the ball but is trying to force mistakes of traveling, poor passing, or any play that gives up possession of the ball.
2. The defensive players should try to force the opposition into hurrying, as loss of poise and poor play will usually result.
3. The defensive team should continually apply pressure but should develop patience for the proper results.
4. The ball should be forced to the sidelines and kept out of the middle of the court as much as possible.

5. Opportunities for double teaming should be exploited as much as possible. The press is a gambling defense.
6. The defensive players should try to force lob or bounce passes but discourage hard, straight passes.
7. Every pass should be challenged.

Player-To-Player Press

Each defensive player has an assigned opponent and must get into position immediately as the press goes into effect. A lapse on the part of one player is enough to defeat the press. The best time to start the press is following a basket, either from the field or the free throw line. The players must assume their positions immediately and should be taught to leave the ball alone as it drops through the basket.

The defensive team is looking for an opportunity to double team and after the first pass is an excellent time. Because of this the player guarding the out-of-bounds opponent will often play loosely and not defend against the first pass but be ready to move to the ball to effect the double team. Occasionally the first pass may be defended in an

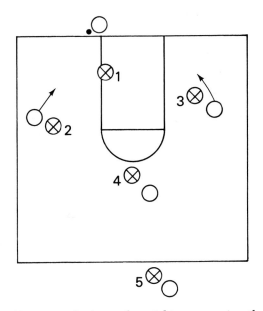

Figure 38. X₁ is overplaying to her right encouraging the ball to be passed to her left. Notice that X₃ is in a tighter defensive position than X₂.

attempt to surprise the opposition and to keep the opponents from knowing what to expect.

The player guarding the throw-in will usually overplay to one side trying to force the pass to go the desired way. The defensive team may decide which way it wants the ball to go on the basis of its personnel or because of the vulnerability of the opposition. Forcing the pass away from the better ball handler would be wise.

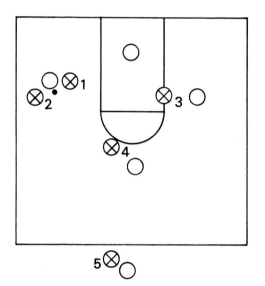

Figure 39. X_2 has prevented the dribble to the outside and X_1 has moved into position to double team.

The defensive team may use several methods of accomplishing the double team. One of these is the jump switch. This would be used if the offensive players cross in attempting to employ the screen.

If the player passing the ball into the court had elected to follow her pass and go behind her teammate for a hand off, X_2 could employ the jump switch. She would switch to the opponent receiving the hand off but not by moving back in a conservative move to stop the drive. Rather she would jump forcing the opponent to turn away from her. The offensive player would have her back to her teammates and be in good position to have the ball tied by X_1.

If the offensive team attempts to move most of its players into its frontcourt and allow the guards to dribble the ball across the center line, the defensive team can still make use of the double team. In

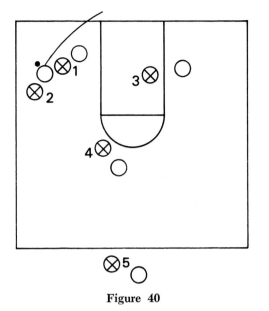

Figure 40

this situation the guards are not so apt to cross but are hoping that the dribbler will be able to move the ball in a one-on-one situation. The player guarding the dribbler will overplay to stop the dribble and turn the opponent in the opposite direction. The other defensive

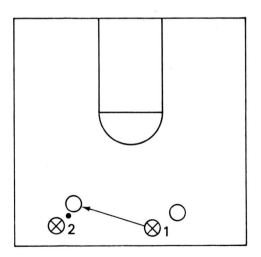

Figure 41. X_2 overplays to her left to force the dribbler to reverse and X_1 leaves her immediate opponent to two time the dribbler.

player will move quickly into the blind side of the dribbler, hoping to effect a surprise double team which will catch the opponent unaware.

If the gamble on a double team fails and the ball is successfully passed, the defensive players should turn and sprint back to help their teammates. If the offensive player is some distance from the basket, the defensive player may trail her hoping to deflect or bat the ball forward to a teammate. An unsuspecting opponent is sometimes vulnerable to a steal in this situation.

As a player is moving the ball down the court with a dribble, the defensive team may want to force the dribbler to use her weaker hand. This is another way of putting pressure on the opponents and forcing a misplay.

The deep defensive players in a player-to-player press should be alert for a long pass. The ball handler usually signals this type of pass by her body position and the backswing of her arm. An alert defense will intercept some of these passes. However, the defensive team must understand that the press is a gamble and sometimes it will be beaten. The defensive players should learn to allow the easy shot when beaten without the desperation play that results in a foul.

TWO-TWO-ONE ZONE PRESS

There are several types of zone presses by original alignment but after the initial pass they tend to resemble each other. The defensive

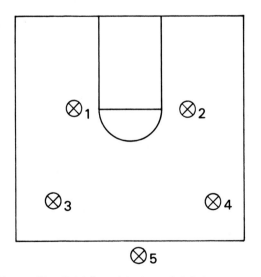

Figure 42. Initial positioning of 2-2-1 zone press.

team does not defend against the first pass except to insure that the ball does not go behind the front line of the defense.

The two front players should remain near the free throw line rather than moving forward to defend the area near the end line. If the first pass goes into this area, the defensive players may threaten to move and harass but should make the opponents come to them. They should keep their hands low and force a high pass. If the first line of defense would move forward near the end line the zone may become overextended and will be more vulnerable. The two front players should try for double teams and if the opponents cross, the defensive players should jump-switch to a double team.

If the ball is passed in to a player who starts to dribble, the front defensive player must stop the sideline dribble. This turns the opponent to the inside where help may be available from the other front player. Some teams that use the zone press try to encourage the offensive team to go to its right, and the personnel of the press is planned for this play. The left front player in the press should be fast to stop the sideline dribble. The second line of defense should float to the ball side trying to maintain good position to intercept.

If the offensive team is successful in making good penetration, the defensive team must retreat at full speed. The use of the voice is important and X_5 is in a position to help direct the play.

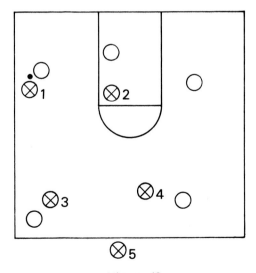

Figure 43

Rebounding

Good defensive rebounding is an extremely important aspect of the game, yet it is often neglected by inexperienced groups. Regardless of the style of defense used, securing the ball following a shot attempt by the opponents is of the utmost importance. Good blocking techniques as discussed in Chapter 2 must be adopted but players must work as a unit in gaining possession of the ball off the backboard.

Two styles of team rebounding have developed. One is an individual system with each defensive player blocking one offensive player. The other starts with the same movement but then abandons the concept of a one-on-one basis and stresses that the players move into good positioning for the rebound. These two systems could be compared to the player-to-player and zone defense. Although the preference of the type of rebounding system chosen might seem to hinge on whether zone or player-to-player defense is used, such is not al-

Defensive Rebounding

ways the case. Players using a zone defense can be taught to block their immediate opponent. Rebounding is somewhat easier in most zone defenses because the players are usually in a closer position to the basket.

After the initial check of the opponent, the players can be taught to forget their opponent and go for the ball. This is emphasizing the positive approach of getting the ball rather than keeping the opponent away. The gaining of the defensive triangle should be stressed so that the team should get all the rebounds except those that move out several feet from the basket. Players must be careful that they do not move too far under the basket and they must learn to combine with teammates so that they are not fighting each other for possession of the ball.

Defense Against the Fast Break

The best defense against the fast break is to get to the backcourt before the opponents do. This can be done by a fast withdrawal by the defense or by aggressive defensive play in the forecourt to stop the first pass away from the basket.

Since the fast break usually starts from a rebound, the opponent who caught the rebound should be momentarily stopped, if possible. This allows time for the defense to retreat into the backcourt before the ball can be moved across the line.

The defensive player who is trying to prevent the outlet pass should play on the outside shoulder of the rebounder. If the rebounder has a middle floor position she should be pressured without an overplay. The purpose of the overplay is to cause difficulties in the pass out to the side and to force a dribble, thus gaining time for her retreating teammates. For the first pass out most teams look to the sideline area near the top of the circle on the side on which the rebound is recovered. A guard should play an intercepting angle on the outlet receiver, forcing her to adjust her position and slowing the initial movement of the fast break.

If the opponents move the ball across the line when there are just two defensive players in the backcourt, these two players must be prepared to cope with the situation. The usual pattern for three-on-two is for the opponent with the ball to move straight down the middle with a teammate on the right and another on the left trying to slip behind the defense. To defend the goal, the two defensive players may choose to play either from a side-by-side position or a front and back position. The side-by-side position is weak because if the opponent with the ball is successful in drawing a defensive player, she will be able to pass to her teammate cutting for the goal. If the offensive player with the ball does not draw one of her two opponents, she can drive between the two for a lay-up. If the two defensive players choose to operate from the one back-one out position, they have a better chance to stop the lay-up.

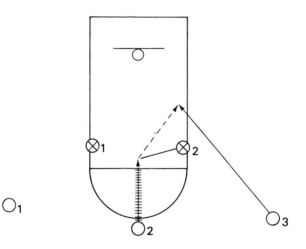

Figure 44. As X_2 moves to stop O_2, O_2 passes to O_3 who then has an unguarded shot.

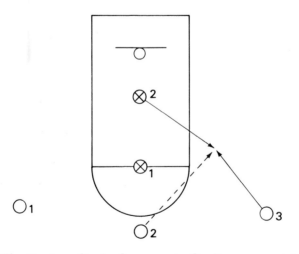

Figure 45. X_1 stops O_2. As O_2 passes to O_3, X_2 moves out to guard the ball and X_1 moves back into deep position.

The front defensive player waits at the free throw line and moves to force the dribbler to pass while her teammate is ready to move toward the pass. (See Figure 45.) As O_2 passes to O_3 and X_2 moves with the pass, X_1 must drop back toward the basket. Some beginners have a tendency to turn their back on the ball in this play and look for the opponent O_1. It is very important that X_1 turns to the inside as she moves back to the deep position so that she is watching the ball and will be ready to deflect or intercept a poor pass. This one-back-one out defensive placement is often called a tandem position.

Defensive Line-up for a Free Throw

The two best rebounders take the inside positions standing as close to the restraining marker as possible. The best rebounder should stand on the side of the more dangerous of the two opponents. The first step should be taken with the foot nearer to the opponent as the rebounder swings into blocking position. The two next best rebounders will line up at the lane crowding the basket side as much as the restraining line permits. One of these two players must block the shooter from the basket. She should step with the foot nearer to the free throw shooter as she moves to block her from the rebound.

Defense for Jump Ball

When taking positions for a jump ball in the opponents' front court, the defensive players' first concern is to be able to stop any shot from a player receiving the tip. The team's defensive strength, therefore, should be between the toss and the basket. If it is obvious that the opponents will not control the tip, these precautions are not so important. Even in this event, there should be one defensive player stationed between the ball and the basket.

The team that gains the tap on a jump ball does not always gain possession of the ball. Clever nonjumpers can be of tremendous value. When a team expects its opponents to get the jump, it may leave one player open in the alignment to encourage the ball to be tapped to her. A player standing behind the opposing jumper can quickly knife in front of the open player and steal the ball from the tip.

Choosing the Defense

When deciding on the proper defense, the teacher of a physical education class or an intramural team, and a coach of an intercholastic team are confronted by very different problems. Inexperienced players, such as one finds in most physical education classes and on many intramural teams, are more successful when they learn one defense well rather than when they use several ineffectively. Beginning players of junior high school age develop better mastery of individual defensive techniques by learning player-to-player defense than by learning zone defense. On the other hand, when a beginning team is faced with inexperienced opponents who are not good ball handlers and cannot shoot from distances greater than 15 feet, it can use a zone defense effectively. This is true even when the defensive players are rather slow moving.

Making a decision about the type of defense for a more experienced team is a more complicated process. Here not only the age, experience, and conditioning of the players but also the amount of practice time available, the number and quality of the substitutes, and the types of offensive play the team will meet must be considered. Perhaps most important of all, the coach must choose a system of defense which best suits the abilities of her players.

The teacher or coach of an experienced group will probably present two or more types of defense because a defense that works against one team may not work against another, or a defense that functioned properly in the first half of the game may not function in the last. In addition, by presenting two or more defenses, the instructor gives the players a better understanding of the game. The more the players know, the more confidence they have as they take the floor against an unknown opponent or face defenses they have used in practice sessions. Well-informed players enjoy the game more as spectators and have a greater appreciation of the skills and strategy involved in the game. Students and players preparing to teach or to coach benefit greatly by learning several systems of play.

Every basketball teacher or coach has developed certain theories about the game. Although a teacher or coach must be flexible in adjusting these theories to differing groups, she must be systematic in planning and presenting her style of game. The players cannot be expected to understand a system of defense if the teacher's presentation is disorganized.

Developing an individual system of defense comes as the result of much experience both as a player and teacher. The wise student of women's basketball does not copy a system but experiments until she develops methods that work well for her. A system of defense that works well for one person or team will not necessarily work best for another. This is the challenge of basketball.

Following is a list of coaching suggestions for defensive play:

1. Learn to which side a player prefers to drive and then overplay her a little to this side.
2. When guarding a player near the base line, overplay a little toward the line. Force her to drive where there is defensive team strength.
3. Try to force the outside pass rather than one toward the basket.
4. Let the ball go out of bounds at the end line rather than trying to knock it back in bounds. The ball may go to an opponent and result in a good shot.
5. Use the voice to help teammates but not to heckle the opposition.
6. Try to analyze the opponent's offensive patterns and be prepared for their maneuvers.

REFERENCES

1. Cousy, Bob, and Power, Frank G., Jr. *Basketball Concepts and Techniques*. Boston: Allyn and Bacon, Inc., 1970.
2. Miller, Kenneth D., and Horky, Rita Jean. *Modern Basketball for Women*. Columbus, Ohio: Charles E. Merrill Co., 1970.
3. Newell, Pete, and Benington, John. *Basketball Methods*. New York: Ronald Press Co., 1962.
4. Redin, Harley. *The Queens Fly High*. Plainview, Texas: Plainview Herald, 1958.
5. Rupp, Adolph. *Championship Basketball*. Englewood Cliffs, N. J.: Prentice-Hall, Inc., 1957.
6. Wilkes, Glenn. *Basketball Coach's Complete Handbook*. Englewood Cliffs, N. J.: Prentice-Hall, Inc., 1962.
7. Wilkes, Glenn. *Winning Basketball Strategy*. Englewood Cliffs, N. J.: Prentice-Hall, Inc., 1959.
8. Wooden, John R. *Practical Modern Basketball*, New York: Ronald Press Co., 1966.

Systems of Offensive Play

There are two distinct types of offensive play, the fast break and ball control. The team that employs the fast break tries to move the ball as quickly as possible to its frontcourt for an easy basket. A team that is more deliberate in moving the ball from the backcourt to the frontcourt is said to use a slow break or ball control style of play.

Fast Break

This type of offensive play requires good ball handling and good team play. Since the fast break is dangerous because the ball may be lost as a result of inaccurate passing, some teams prefer to use it very rarely. However, there are definite advantages other than the obvious possibility of the cheap basket. The fast break pressures the other team into dropping back quickly on defense. Since one or both of the guards may start to drop back, they cut their team's rebounding power. When using the fast break, the offense also can move the ball to the scoring area before the opponents can organize a press defense. By scoring easy baskets, a team can demoralize its opposition.

Although the fast break is accomplished most easily from an interception made near the center line and from this position any team has the jump on its opponents, a team cannot count on making many pass interceptions and must be able to run the fast break from a rebound. The player getting the rebound tries to move the ball out fast, usually to the side on which she caught the rebound.

As the rebounder gets possession of the ball she should call "ball" so the four teammates start moving to designated positions. Some clever rebounders will be able to make the outlet pass before landing from the rebound. However, this is quite difficult and most players will wait until their feet are under them to make the pass. The rebounder must pivot to the outside as she tries to locate her teammate and the defensive positioning of her opponents. The quickness of making the initial pass is very important to the fast break, but a turnover resulting from a poor pass would be disastrous and rebounders must learn the necesssity of eliminating turnovers from this play. The rebounder may use a dribble to move the ball away from the basket if she has trouble getting the pass away quickly.

Teams may choose to use various positionings in running the fast break, but the usual plan is to have the strong side guard move to the side and receive the outlet pass. The weak side guard would take the middle position and the weak side forward the far sideline position.

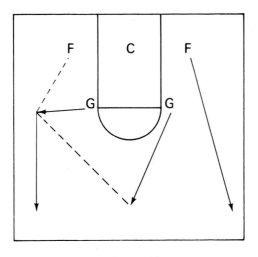

Figure 46

In Figure 46 the forward who got the rebound passed to the near guard who had moved to the side. After the guard passed to the weak side guard breaking to the middle, she filled one side passing lane and the weak side forward took the other.

The teacher might be wise to stress that the receiver of the outlet pass should be motionless as she waits for the pass. She is a better target for the rebounder than if she is moving and the receiver will find her job a little easier as well. This guard must move quickly to get to the sideline to be waiting in position for the outlet pass. As teams become more proficient in handling the ball on the fast break, the receiver may be moving since she would be able to execute the play more quickly.

In running the fast break the team wants to get three players going down the floor full speed with the one in the middle handling the ball. Filling all three lanes is important and players must be very alert to gain these positions immediately.

When the team has achieved the 3-on-2 situation, it should move the ball straight toward the basket in an effort to draw an opponent. At this point it is best for the player with the ball to dribble toward the head of the circle while two teammates break, one on the right side and one on the left. This gives the player with the ball a chance to pass in either direction. If the player is on the left side of the court with two teammates to her right, she obviously has only one direction in which to pass the ball.

At the beginning of this play, if the two defensive players are standing side-by-side, the dribbler should start between them. If neither moves to stop her, the offensive player should drive between them for a lay-up. If one of the defensive players moves to stop the dribbler, she should pass to her teammate who is cutting from that side. (See Figure 47.)

If the defensive players assume a one out-one back position, it is more difficult to get a lay-up, but a close shot should be possible.

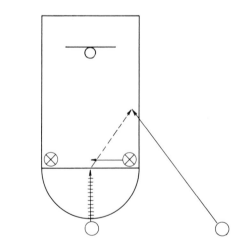

Figure 47. The left defensive player moves to stop dribbler who passes to her teammate cutting behind the opponent.

(See Figure 48.) A fourth teammate should follow the ball handler down the floor in a trailing position. If the defense is able to thwart the fast break, the trailer may be open for a short shot. The fifth player should remain in the backcourt ready to play defensively in case of an interception.

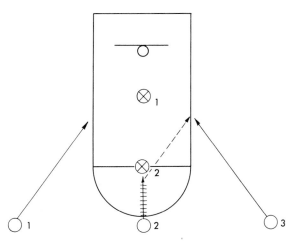

Figure 48. X_2 stops the dribble of O_2 who passes to O_3. As X_1 moves with the pass, X_2 will probably drop back under the basket. O_3 has an option. She can bounce pass to O_1 who is breaking on the left side of the basket or she can pass to O_2 at the free throw line for a set shot.

To know what a fast break is and to know how it is executed is not enough. Following are several requirements any team must meet in order to master a successful fast break.
1. A team must develop good defensive rebounding because it must get possession of the ball before it can start a fast break.
2. Players must be able to pass accurately while moving at full speed. If a team does not have this skill, it cannot use the fast break.
3. Offensive players must be aware of the positions of the opponents and how to maneuver to take advantage of their numerical superiority. Such awareness is developed by practicing several possible situations.
4. Players must be able to shoot while driving at top speeds.
5. The team must be in good physical condition.
6. Players must have the judgment to keep from taking a poor percentage shot when the opponents have thwarted the fast break.

Ball Control

If a player is not successful in attempting a shot from the fast break or if the team has chosen to bring the ball across the line slowly, the team must set up a formation and pattern of play that may outwit its opponents. This deliberate maneuvering is called ball control, and many patterns of play can be employed.

Cutting

One such pattern uses the cut or break, one of the basic maneuvers in basketball. In order for the offense to employ it successfully, the players must have good body balance and reaction time. They must be able to deceive with feints and make quick stops and starts if they want to be successful in losing their opponents. The team members must also work together so that two players do not cut into the same place simultaneously. One of the mistakes which beginning teams make is to have several teammates cutting at the same time; the middle of the court therefore is always "jammed," and no player is free to receive a pass.

The give-and-go is a fundamental basketball play which makes use of the cut. It received its name because a player "gives" the ball to a teammate and immediately "goes" for the basket. In the simplest variation of the give-and-go, a player passes to a teammate, breaks free from her opponent to receive a return pass, and is in position for an easy lay-up shot.

Beginning players need to be impressed with the importance of watching the teammate for the cut when they receive the ball. Often they are so concerned with their own possibilities that they forget to concentrate on the movements of their teammates. Since the give-and-go has many variations, it can be used as a continuously moving cutting offense. (See Figure 49.)

Screen

The screen is usually incorporated in such plays. In the play illustrated in Figure 50 as O_5 started a cut for the basket, O_2 could have passed to her and then cut behind her. O_5 holds her position until O_2 is free for a shot. O_5 then moves for the rebound.

Another type of screen play is to have O_5 set the screen on the player guarding O_2 as illustrated in Figure 51. After the screen is set, O_2 can start her drive. The player guarding O_2 may try to fight her way out of the screen or she may get help from X_5. If the defensive players switch, then O_5 should roll from the screen to receive a pass from O_2.

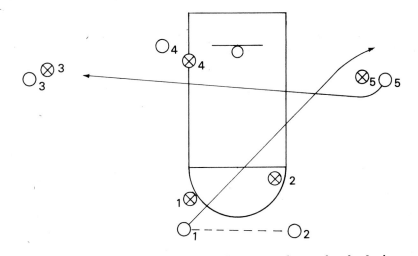

Figure 49. O_1 passes to O_2 and makes an inside cut for the basket. O_2 has the option of passing or waiting. If O_1 does not receive the pass, she continues behind O_5. O_5 cuts toward the basket and O_2 may pass or wait. If O_5 does not receive the pass, she continues into the area of O_3, as O_3 moves into the spot held previously by O_1. The entire play is ready to be rerun, this time with O_2 passing the ball and making the first cut.

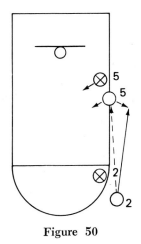

Figure 50

Another possibility for this pattern is to have O_5 move into screening position for O_3. (See Figure 49.)

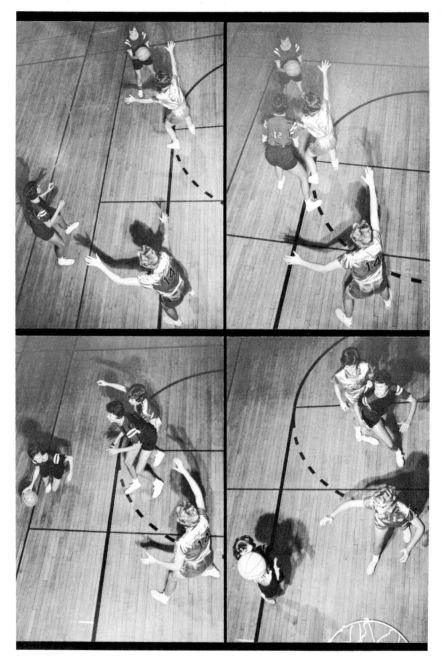

Screen Play When Guards Do Not Switch

Screen Play When Guards Switch

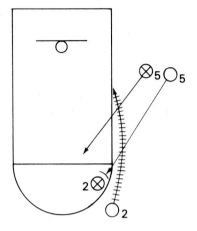

Figure 51. O₅ sets the screen on X₂, and O₂ drives for a lay-up.

Pivot Player

There are many successful styles of offense. Many teams use a pivot player on offense, and the use of a pivot can lead to excellent offensive play. In fact, some persons feel that a pivot player is essential. A team using a pivot would like a talented player to fill that position. Preferably, she should be a tall, agile, deceptive, resourceful shooter because she will be closely guarded. She should be able to execute several shots and will be much more effective if she can shoot while moving either to her right or left. In addition to her scoring responsibilities she will be used to set up plays for teammates by screening or feeding a cutting player. Finding such a player is only one of the problems with this style of play.

Moving the ball to the pivot player requires skillful passing, and the bounce and two hand overhead passes are two of the most useful methods. If the team is good at outside shooting which draws the defensive players out, it gives more space in which to pass the ball to the pivot. If the pivot player uses the area near the basket and almost out to the free throw line, she is in low post position. If she stations herself at the free throw line, she is in high post position. In low post position, the pivot player is in a much better shooting area, but this area is easier than the high post spot for her opponents to defend.

If the pivot is playing a high post position, she does not have to worry about violating the three second lane rule, and she is in an excellent position to hand off to cutting teammates. Two such possible plays to run against a player-to-player defense are hand offs to a player breaking from the side or to a teammate from the criss-cross pattern as in Figures 52 and 53.

Another play which can be run from the high post position against a player-to-player defense is a pass to the pivot from an outside player who cuts to one side of the post, then reverses to the other side. This forces the opponent guarding the outside player into a position where it is impossible for her to follow her player. If the pivot faces the

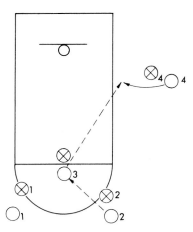

Figure 52. O_2 passes to O_3 who passes to O_4 cutting for the basket.

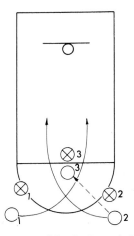

Figure 53. O_2 passes to O_3 and both O_2 and O_1 break for the basket. The pass can go to either O_1 or O_2.

basket she is in a position to shoot or drive if her guard moves to the free player who is cutting for the basket. (See page 95.)

If the pivot plays from a low post position, she must be careful to time her moves into the lane to coincide with the pass opportunities of her teammates. The pivot player should break toward the player with the ball. She would be moving toward the oncoming pass rather than away from it. The pivot should start her movement across the lane as the anticipated passer receives the ball. Since it is quite difficult to feed the pivot from a position directly at the head of the lane, the two offensive players positioned at the head of the circle should play to the right and left of the circle.

When the pass goes to the pivot player, she should shoot if she is open. She should also look for teammates who are cutting or who are open for set shots. If she is being closely guarded by an opponent using the player-to-player defense, she must keep moving to work herself into a position for a pass. If the opponent plays in front of her, the pivot must circle around to get position on her guard. If the opponent plays on the side and slightly ahead of her, she should turn her back to her guard and hold her hand high for a touchdown type pass. (See page 96.) Since the pivot player is playing near the basket, she should develop into a strong rebounder. A quick shot after the rebound provides a scoring opportunity for players in this position.

Double Pivot

Some teams use two pivots in their offensive style of play. The two pivot players may choose to play with one in the high position and the other in the low post spot. The player operating from the low post may try to slip behind the defense as well as maneuver into the usual law post position. Other teams set up in an offensive formation with two players in high post position, one at each side of the lane. They must learn to play together and can use many screening plays.

Weave

The weave is a type of offensive play designed to pull the guards away from the basket or to lull them into complacency by repeating the same pattern over and over. During the weave an offensive player should make a move for the basket as soon as she sees an opportunity. But the weave does not provide a very strong scoring threat; it is used

Pivot Play

Rolling Against Pivot Guard

most frequently when a team is ahead and wants to run out the clock. Also the weave is quite ineffective against a zone in any situation other than a stall.

The weave can be run by three, four, or five players. The ball handling ability of the players would be one of the factors determining how many players to use in the weave. Some centers lack both agility and the ball handling ability to play outside. Moving the center outside may weaken the rebounding ability of a team to the point that it is a poor gamble. Since the shot from a weave offense is often not anticipated, this style of offense may result in poor offensive rebounding.

The weave, illustrated in Figure 54, must be started by one of the two inside players, O_2 or O_3. The dribbler should always move to the inside to provide a screen for the oncoming teammate. The ball should be handed to the new dribbler and the teammates should pass close to one another. The dribbler should use the outside hand for better ball protection and also for an easier hand off. One possibility of scoring from the weave is to have the player O_1 start to move for the ball and then make a quick cut toward the basket. If X_1 had started to follow the first movement of O_1, she might be left behind.

Another possibility is for O_3 to drive around O_2 and go for the basket. If her opponent is a little slow, she may succeed in getting free for a shot.

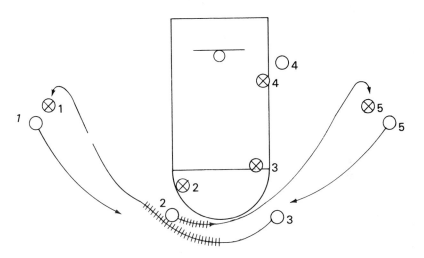

Figure 54. O_2 starts dribbling the ball and hands off to O_3 who is cutting behind her. O_3 dribbles and passes to O_1 who dribbles back toward the head of the circle and hands off to O_5. This entire pattern is repeated.

Overloading a Zone

If the opponents are using a zone defense, the offensive players should station two of their players in a zone covered by one opponent. If they pass the ball quickly, the defensive player will have difficulty moving fast enough to guard both of these players, and one of them should get an unguarded set shot. The placement of the players involved in the overload is quite important. Players attacking a zone should stand at the cracks or seams of a zone. The seam is the area of overlap between two defensive players. (See Figures 55 and 56.) It is important for the offensive team to understand how the zone is shifting in order to station its players in the most advantageous spots. It is wise also to choose the team's best set shooters to overload the zone.

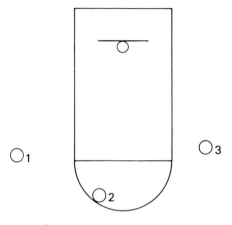

Figure 55. Suggested placement for overloading zone which uses a two player front.

Figure 56. Suggested placement for overloading zone which uses a one player front.

Offense Against the Press

Since pressure defenses have become more common, a team must be ready to attack this defense. The preparation should include both theorizing and practice. The players should understand that structurally the press is the weakest defense in basketball. It attempts to do in the full court area what it is difficult to do within twenty feet of the basket. Since the press attempts double-teaming and overplaying, it leaves openings in areas away from the ball that are very vulnerable. A team that plays with poise and intelligence can discourage this type of defense.

A speedy pass in following a basket by the opponents may get the ball in play before the defense is set. If attacking a player-to-player press, the best plan may be to give the ball to the best dribbler and allow her to bring the ball to the frontcourt by herself. Most good dribblers have little trouble in a one-on-one situation. If the best dribbler has a very strong defensive opponent, the ball could be given to the player who has the weakest opponent.

When attacking the zone press, a team should try to keep the ball in the middle of the court. When players are double-teamed near the sideline, the sideline becomes a third player. If the dribbler is being double-teamed she should never turn her back on her own basket. Players should avoid crossing in the backcourt as this invites double teams. They should stay spread and try to beat the front line of the zone. Once the zone is penetrated the offense should move quickly trying to gain a numerical superiority over the defense. Players must move to meet passes, as failing to do so often results in an interception. The dribble is less useful than against a player-to-player press, but it can be helpful once the ball has passed the front line. It can be used to drive to the basket, to lure the defense into a double team, and to avoid trouble when no teammate seems to be open. One teammate should stay behind the ball for an outlet pass in case her teammate with the ball gets in trouble.

When a player is pressured behind the end line she should remember that she has five seconds to make the pass. She can run along the line or request a time-out. Players being double-teamed sometimes forget that a jump ball is much less disastrous than an interception with teammates in poor defensive positioning.

Jump Ball

Planning the strategy for jump balls can be very helpful to a team. The diamond line-up is probably the most common, although the box or others can also be used. Usually the best receiver would be facing the jumper in spot B.

If the tip goes to B she can feed to C or D cutting for the basket. The safest way to tip the ball may be back to E if the defense has left E open. This is most apt to happen in a team's forecourt.

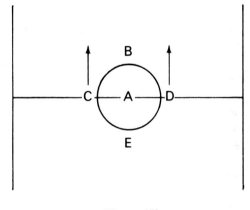

Figure 57

Choosing the Offensive System of Play

For a beginning physical education class, the teacher will probably base her choice of offense on the system of defense she has chosen to teach. If she has presented zone defense to the class, she will not have much success teaching a cutting offense. If she taught a player-to-player defense, she has no reason to teach overloading a zone. By a process of elimination she will finally choose which offense to present to her class. The teacher of an intermediate or advanced class usually presents a variety of offensive play possibilities, and she scales that variety to the age and experience of her students.

The basketball coach generally has to consider many other factors such as team personnel, practice time, and opposing teams' defenses before she can decide on which systems of offense to teach. For example, if she has no player proficient as a pivot, she may be wise to use other styles of offense. If her team will play many other teams, she has to teach offenses suitable against both player-to-player and zone defenses.

There are some principles of offensive play used against a player-to-player defense that differ from those used against zone defense. Since the defensive players follow their individual opponents when using a player-to-player defense, the offensive players' most successful attack is to outrun or outmaneuver their opponents. In such a situation with speed and agility to be considered, a cutting and screening game is effective, or a team could use a pivot player successfully. Some teams might choose a double pivot hoping that the opponents do not have two strong pivot guards. If this proves true the pivot guarded by the weak opponent should stay in the post position the majority of the time. If the defensive players are not in very good condition, the offensive team can keep moving and play a fast game hoping to outlast the opponents.

A team may find the concept of clear outs to be helpful. If one of the offensive players leaves her usual area of operation, she provides a greater space in which her teammate may maneuver. A forward may vacate her area hoping that the guard will be able to drive for a good shot.

Offensive players also have to be trained to study the play of the opponents and to determine their habits of switching assignments. As a result the offensive team sometimes can force a switch which puts a short defensive player on a tall player, or if there is one opponent who is noticeably weaker than the others, it can feed the teammate who is being guarded by the weak opponent. If it finds the defensive players use a sinking defense that collapses on the pivot, the offense can shoot set shots and screen and drive from the outside.

While cutting and running by offensive players proves successful against player-to-player defense, it is not effective against the zone defense which changes position with the movement of the ball. In addition, while moving the ball quickly brings about an opening for a cut or a good set shot and might be more successful, the best offense against a zone is to score consistently with long shots. If a team is successful with shots of 20 to 22 feet, the zone has to be abandoned. Since this kind of shooting is difficult for many teams, however, other offensive maneuvers must be used.

If the zone defense leaves openings in the center of the floor, the offense should cut from the outside and attempt to pass the ball into the zone. A good zone makes this difficult, but the offensive players should be alert and try all possibilities. The offensive team must be aware that the placement of the attacking players is important. They should be stationed at the edge of a zone rather than in the center. In all cases, fast passing is essential to outmaneuver the zone.

When playing against a zone, the offensive team should try to determine the most effective rebounder of the opposing team. The best rebounder of the offensive team can then be placed in the area of the weakest rebounding opponents. Plays can then be directed to the side of the floor where the strong rebounder is stationed in an effort to pull her away from the basket. This maneuver gives the offensive team the double advantage of having its strongest rebounder in a good position and the best defensive rebounder away from the basket.

Another method of attack is to run the majority of plays into the zone of the weakest defensive player. The screen can be very helpful against a zone. One such play is illustrated in Figure 58.

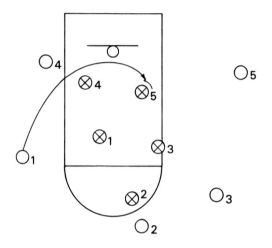

Figure 58. O_1 moves to set a screen on X_5. O_2 passes the ball to O_5 who moves in for a shot.

A team should take every opportunity to fast break against a zone defense. If it is able to get into its frontcourt before the zone is set, it has the defense at a disadvantage.

When playing against a press, the offensive players must remember they are going for a basket as well as trying to move the ball. A long touchdown type pass may give them a lay-up shot. The press is vulnerable to this kind of play and to ignore it is to play into the hands of the defense.

The speed of the attack is an important consideration of offensive play. How deliberate should the team be in moving the ball and how sure of a shot before it is attempted? The team's rebounding strength, ability to shoot, the score and number of fouls, all affect this decision. If a team is being out rebounded, it should wait for a high percentage shot. If part of the strategy is to outrun the other team, a very deliberate attack is of little help. If a team is behind, it must keep shooting to score, but once it has gained an advantage, it should be careful about giving the ball away on a relatively poor shot.

Any offensive pattern should capitalize on the abilities of the players. Plays should be planned so that the best shooter takes the shot, and the best rebounder is under the basket. If a screen is needed, the player who executes a screen most effectively should fill that role, and the best passer should be handling the ball. This should not be true all of the time because all players should think of themselves as potential scorers. It is certainly desirable to have the opponents think of all the offensive players as potential scorers, but such an impression is difficult to create if the team does not use them in this role.

An offensive system must be flexible enough to allow individual players to use their abilities in a one-on-one situation. If an offensive player can beat her immediate opponent by superior skill, she certainly has helped strengthen the total team offense, and she should be encouraged. A good set shooter, a scoring pivot, or a fast starting driver can be threats that also strengthen the total offense. Only a coordinated attack that employs all the individual abilities achieves full scoring potential, and each player, no matter how successful, must think of herself as just one part of the attack and continue to play as part of the team.

Such good team offense tries to spread the defense, works for the easy shot, gets the rebound for a second shot, and has balanced floor play. The weave is a useful device to teach a balance in attack since each player is so dependent on the other's moves. The weave also emphasizes the necessity of strength under the backboard. Because of the glaring lack of positioning for rebounds in the weave, playing the weave should make players more aware of the importance of offensive rebounding. Since beginning players often shoot without any awareness of where their teammates are playing, they should be taught that one or more teammates should be in rebounding position for every shot.

The offensive team should use an offensive rebounding triangle in trying to get inside the defensive ring around the backboard. Offensive rebounding requires a good deal of skill because in the majority of situations the opponent has blocked the path to the basket. The offensive player should make use of the fake and may find a double fake valuable in getting around an opponent. The offensive player has the advantage of knowing the offensive patterns and shooting habits of her team, and she should make every effort to get into a position to rebound by anticipating the shot.

For good offensive floor position, a team must always have one player free for an outlet pass. If a player is double teamed and has nowhere to go, she should be able to back out of trouble by passing the ball out to a teammate to start another offensive maneuver. This also puts an offensive player in a position to drop back immediately on defense to stop a fast break if the opponents suddenly gain possession of the ball.

Although the usual offensive line-up is the two guards away from the basket with the three bigger players playing under the basket,

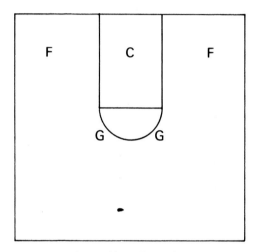

Figure 59.   Two-Three

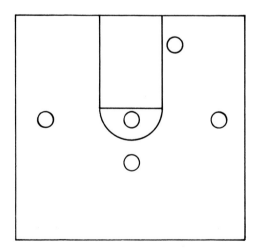

Figure 60.   One-Three-One

other offensive formations have developed. In some cases the different placement of players has brought about new names rather than the traditional guard, forward, and center. The one-three-one has resulted in the term "wing."

One of the newer offensive formations is called the stack offense with four of the five players standing at the free throw line facing each other as in the shooting of a free throw attempt.

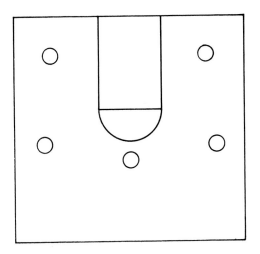

Figure 61. Three-Two

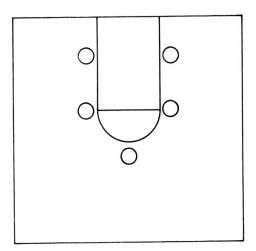

Figure 62. One-Two-Two. The two low post players could flare into corner positions.

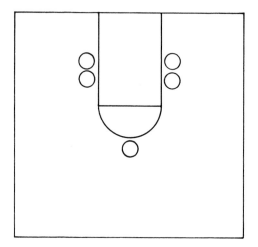

Figure 63.   Stack Offense.

Many classes and teams playing at the beginning and intermediate levels will operate from the traditional two-three formation. This is the alignment that is seen most often and best understood, and successful plays can be run against both player-to-player and zone defenses. This formation uses the center as a pivot player. In a situation where no pivot player is available, the three-two might be used. The weave lends itself to this floor positioning.

If a team has two players who can operate in the pivot position, it might use the one-three-one with the pivots playing a tandem position. The offensive positioning illustrated in Figures 62 and 63 could also be used with the pivot players, the ones farthest from the basket. A team that uses two pivots in tandem formation will probably be more successful if the two players can alternate roles.

The teacher or coach must choose an offense that seems best for her. There is no one successful style of offensive basketball. The teacher or coach must keep in mind the abilities of her players.

One of the first questions a leader of a basketball group has to answer is how much should the players follow set play patterns and how much should they be allowed to free lance. To allow either a class or a highly skilled team to operate an offense without any planned play patterns is to reduce their effectiveness and to misuse an educational opportunity for the development of the players. However, to require players to use nothing but set patterns may make the play so mechanical that it is easily defended. The limiting of individual freedom and initiative can become stifling and contribute to lack of enthusiasm and to staleness.

The coach or teacher should help players understand the purposes of their movements so that they can make adjustments to the defense. A good offense must be a thinking offense and attack the defense intelligently. Every adjustment by the defense should bring a counter-adjustment by the offense.

The coach and teacher of basketball must resist the temptation to make the offense too complex. A team will perform much more effectively if it does simple things well rather than if it tries many plays that are not well executed. How much players can absorb will depend on several factors such as ability, experience, motivation, intelligence, and length of unit or season. The mistake of trying to do too much in too short a time is more common than attempting too little, and is probably a more serious error to rectify.

One of the principles of offensive play sometimes overlooked is the importance of the movements of the players off the ball. This is especially true when operating against a player-to-player defense. If the weak side players just stand and do nothing, this permits the opponents to turn their attention elsewhere. Players must learn the importance of keeping their opponents "entertained." Feints, draws, and cuts that do nothing but force the concentration of the defense away from the main action are an important part of offensive basketball.

The coach or teacher should consider the correlation of the defense to the offense in reaching a decision about the type of offense to use. The use of a two-three zone may aid the fast break, while running the fast break from a player-to-player defense may be more difficult especially for inexperienced teams. However, a team that uses a pressing player-to-player defense may find itself attuned to fast aggressive play on both ends of the court.

The tempo of the game has a great deal to do with the final outcome. This is a factor that is often slighted by inexperienced students of the game. Every person has an optimum speed at which she performs. Although this can change somewhat from day to day depending on fatigue and emotional factors, a person has developed habits of movement that are not easily shaken. If a person is forced into playing at a different speed than is her norm, she often has a serious adjustment problem. The wise coach knows this and will plan her offense to fit the tempo of her players. Furthermore, she will spend considerable practice time in working on offensive plays at the desired tempo. But, if the coach is really wise, she will practice playing contests at different speeds. All good players must be capable of playing a fast aggressive style of ball as well as a more deliberate ball control kind of game. Each can be useful. Either can be used to upset an opponent.

In developing an offensive system a coach or teacher must look for overall team balance. This includes floor balance, shooting balance, rebounding balance, and even balance of defensive positioning in the event of the loss of the ball. This requires a well-organized system, good instruction, hours of concentrated practice, and a wise blend of the abilities of the participants.

Coaching suggestions for offensive play:

1. Send a player without the ball through the lane. If an opponent follows her she should call "Man-to-Man," if no opponent follows her she should call "Zone." Now the offense knows how to attack.
2. Teach the offense to keep the ball in motion. It will be easier to attack a defense which has to stay in motion than a static defense concentrated in the scoring area.
3. Teach the offense to work for the high percentage shot.
4. Train the offense to try for a second shot.
5. Teach the offense to analyze the defense. Teach them to understand how the opponents move and how to force the opponents into less desirable positions.

REFERENCES

1. Cousy, Bob, and Power, Frank G., Jr. *Basketball Concepts and Techniques.* Boston: Allyn and Bacon, Inc., 1970.
2. Miller, Kenneth D., and Horky, Rita Jean. *Modern Basketball for Women.* Columbus, Ohio: Charles E. Merrill Co., 1970.
3. McGuire, Frank. *Offensive Basketball.* Englewood Cliffs, N. J.: Prentice-Hall, Inc., 1958.
4. Neal, Patsy. *Basketball Techniques for Women.* New York: Ronald Press Co., 1966.
5. Newell, Pete, and Benington, John. *Basketball Methods.* New York: Ronald Press Co., 1962.
6. Redin, Harley. *The Queens Fly High.* Plainview, Texas: Plainview Herald, 1958.
7. Wilkes, Glenn. *Basketball Coach's Complete Handbook.* Englewood Cliffs, N. J.: Prentice-Hall, Inc., 1962.
8. Wilkes, Glenn. *Winning Basketball Strategy.* Englewood Cliffs, N. J.: Prentice-Hall, Inc., 1959.

Chapter 6

Suggestions for Planning Basketball Units of Instruction

In this chapter three units are presented which could be used for a high school or college basketball class. Each unit is planned to include material for about 25 or 30 lessons. Since the third unit may be a little advanced for the high school level, the high school teacher might want to combine activities of the second and third units.

In order that the student can develop game sense, she must practice offensive and defensive skills in a game situation. Game play should start rather early in the unit, and skill practice and game play should continue throughout the course of instruction. In the beginning days of the unit, skill practice should occupy the larger share of the daily time allotment, but skill practice should gradually decrease until game play takes the greater portion of the class period. In this way the two are learned together. Practice of skills, without the opportunity to use the skill in a game, can be frightfully monotonous and unrewarding. Repeated lessons of game play alone can cease to be challenging, and players may make the same mistakes repeatedly. Game play can be a source of motivation for improving fundamental skills; skill practice and game play must go together.

If permanent teams are established early in the unit, better team play can be expected than if team membership constantly changes. Players must practice and play together in order to understand coordinated movement.

Most students of basketball feel that it is far wiser to have inexperienced players learn a player-to-player defense before starting on a zone. Using a player-to-player defense helps stress good individual techniques. Since a player's individual responsibilities are easier to determine in a nonswitching player-to-player defense, most girls will find it easier to understand and accept their mistakes with this system.

Another factor in determining what defense to use would be the type of offense that a teacher would like to stress. Since most beginning classes will be working on cutting, the lay-up, and other short shots, the player-to-player defense is ideal for testing the offense. Beginners working against a zone will find little opportunity to cut or to shoot the lay-up, so there will be little relationship between the skill practice and game play.

One of the reasons advanced for the teaching of zone defenses at the eighth and ninth grade level is that the game play is more orderly. Beginning players using a player-to-player defense can produce a disorganized, rough type of game with lots of turnovers in which the players may become frantic in their efforts. When contrasted with this hectic type of playing frequently associated with a player-to-player defense, the teams using a zone defense seem much more organized. Upon closer examination of why the class using a zone defense seems more orderly, one is apt to find little action. The players dribble the ball uncontested into the forecourt and pass the ball around the periphery of the zone. The players are not skilled in shooting over the zone and do not know how to penetrate it. The scores of such games are usually very low.

Usually much more action occurs with inexperienced players using a player-to-player defense. This provides a better laboratory for learning. The teacher of beginning classes will need much patience. Players should be encouraged to be daring and aggressive but to use good judgment and body control. This requires both practice and guidance, and there is no short cut to acquiring the ability to play basketball.

One of the problems associated with the teaching of basketball in the public schools is the lack of facilities for the number of students. If a teacher has one gym for thirty to forty students, the amount of activity and learning that takes place is apt to be less than with a better ratio. Since a game of basketball requires just ten students, the teacher's problem will be how to give all students a chance to play. The fact that the player-to-player defense requires more movement by both the offense and the defense would be an advantage in this situation as far as reaching the physiological objectives of the class.

The use of half-court basketball is recommended for large classes. If two cross courts are available, forty students could be playing simultaneously. Ten students would play at each of the four side baskets.

Official rules apply with one modification. If the defensive team intercepts or rebounds the ball, it must take the ball past the head of the circle before it attempts a shot for the basket. Shooting for the basket prior to this becomes a violation.

There are times when a teacher is wise to give individual students some special attention. If one or two of the ninth grade students are ready to start the jump shot, the teacher should find a time to present the skill to them. The better students should be challenged with more advanced skills if they have already mastered the techniques presented to the class as a whole.

Beginning Unit

Skills:

Teach the students all of the following:
1. Catching
2. Chest pass
3. One hand underhand pass
4. One hand push shot
5. Catching and throwing while moving
6. Stationary lay-up
7. Guarding stance and slide
8. Dribble
9. Moving lay-up
10. Guarding a player with the ball
11. Front pivot
12. Two hand underhand pass
13. One hand overhand pass
14. Chest shot
15. One-on-one
16. Feint
17. Player-to-player defense
18. Rebounding
19. Guarding player without the ball
20. Cutting
21. Bounce pass
22. Two-on-one
23. Underhand free throw

Offensive Concepts:

Teach students to:
1. Move to meet a pass
2. Create spaces

3. Cut into a space
4. Move the ball to the sideline and away from opponents' goal when in the backcourt
5. Keep the ball moving
6. Try for a high percentage shot
7. Follow the shot for the rebound
8. Shoot only when in a balanced position
9. Use variety in attack
10. Develop deception

Defensive Concepts:

Teach students to:
1. Stay between opponent and basket
2. Maintain a defensive position rather than moving out for a possible interception
3. Stay three feet away from opponent with the ball to prevent a drive
4. Block out on rebounds
5. Jump to block a shot only when opponent leaves floor
6. Guard loosely when opponent is far from basket; guard closely when opponent is near basket
7. Drop back quickly into the backcourt when the ball is lost in the frontcourt
8. Guard opponent a little closer after opponent has dribbled
9. Be alert for interception and tie balls
10. Avoid fouling

Intermediate Unit

Skills:

After review of the beginning unit, present the following:
1. Zone defense (2-3)
2. Two hand overhead pass
3. Rear pivot
4. Screen
5. Jumping for tossed ball
6. Hook pass
7. Hook shot
8. Overloading a zone
9. Down the middle lay-up

10. Three-on-two
11. Fast break

Offensive Concepts:

Teach students to:
1. Move the ball faster than the guards can shift in order to beat a zone
2. Watch the movement of the defense and take advantage of its mistakes
3. Use long shots to draw the defense away from the basket
4. Move the ball quickly across the center line before the defensive team has formed a zone
5. Use the bounce pass to avoid an opponent
6. Understand the use of the screen

Defensive Concepts:

Teach the students to:
1. Block the passing lanes between the ball and the basket
2. Observe opponents and note if they always drive to the same side, shoot a certain shot, etc.
3. Analyze offensive patterns and learn to expect what the opponents will do
4. Try to combat a screen by moving around it
5. Combine with teammates in going for a rebound; do not fight own player for the ball
6. Never move away from the basket if opponents have a 3 on 2 situation

Advanced Unit

Skills:

After a review of the beginning and intermediate units, present:
1. Player-to-player defense
2. Zone defense (2-3)
3. Two hand shoulder pass
4. Two hand overhead shot
5. Roll (combined with screen)
6. Jump shot
7. Crossover lay-up
8. Press
9. Pivot player moves

Offensive Concepts:

Teach students to:

1. Use a cutting and screening offense against a player-to-player defense
2. Use fast passing and set shots against a zone defense
3. Never let a pressure defense be upsetting; be poised
4. Use the long "touchdown" pass
5. Learn some of the plays that can be used with a pivot player
6. Develop some original plays

BASKETBALL INCIDENCE CHART

NAME Sue Jones   DATE Jan. 7

OFFENSIVE SKILLS	1	2	TOTAL (1-2)
PASSING	SUCCESSFUL ＃Ｌ	UNSUCCESSFUL ∣	4
CATCHING	SUCCESSFUL ＃Ｌ ∣∣∣	FUMBLED ∣	7
SHOOTING	SUCCESSFUL ∣	UNSUCCESSFUL ∣	0
PIVOTING	SUCCESSFUL ∣	ALLOWED TIE BALL	1
DRIBBLING	SUCCESSFUL ∣∣	ILLEGAL	2
		TRAVELING ∣	−1
REBOUNDING	∣		1
FOULING		∣	−1
DEFENSIVE SKILLS		TOTAL OFFENSE	13
	INTERCEPTED BALL		0
	TIED BALL ∣		1
	BLOCKED SHOT ∣	ALLOWED SHOT ∣	0
	REBOUND ∣∣		2
		FOUL	0
		TOTAL DEFENSE	3
		TOTAL	16

Figure 64. Incidence Chart.

Defensive Concepts:

Teach students to:

1. Realize that a zone defense should be used against a team that uses cuts, screens, and a pivot player
2. Realize that a player-to-player defense should be used against a team with good set shooting
3. Understand the importance of stopping the pass to the pivot player by using team effort
4. Learn the advantages and disadvantages of double teaming
5. Learn the principles of when a switch is advisable when using a player-to-player defense
6. Be aware of advantages and disadvantages of a press defense and recognize situations when it would be helpful

The teacher or coach may find that the keeping of charts or records assists in the learning process of the players. The frequently used incidence chart can be kept easily by the players sitting on the sidelines. If a player who is observing is forced to watch the action of the game very carefully and to make judgments about plays, she will increase her knowledge of game play. At the same time, the tabulation which she makes of a player's performance should aid that player's evaluation of her effectiveness in the game. Since players tend to remember their successful shots better than the many times they gave away the ball in futile scoring attempts, the incidence charts can be effective reminders of mistakes made during a game. The charts indicate group weaknesses as well as individual mistakes. Finally, the charts can be used by students and teachers to analyze play, to indicate areas of needed practice, and to motivate players to improve in fundamental skills.

Another way to evaluate the shooting ability of a team or its individual members is to use a game shot chart. Each legal shot attempt is noted on a chart of a basketball floor plan. The number of the player attempting the shot is recorded in the same relative position of the court from which the shot was attempted. If the shot is good, the number is circled. Letters can be used beside the number to denote the type of shot: J for jump; H for hook; P for push. The position of the player recorded on this chart also indicates the offensive patterns and the success of the defense.

It appears that this team plans its attack for the right side of the floor. The opponents might overshift slightly to this side.

Keeping a record of rebounds and assists is a useful device which provides the basis for evaluations of a player's effectiveness in a game. Some teachers and coaches prefer using a shot chart plus a record of rebounds and assists rather than the more cumbersome incidence chart.

Other devices a teacher can use to motivate students are having students shoot 25 or 50 free throws each day and record the number made; using the jump and reach test to measure a player's jump[1]; or using the 30 second shooting test[2] at the beginning and end of a unit.

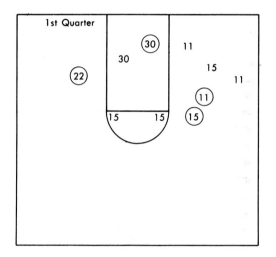

Figure 65. Shot Chart.

A teacher or coach should always be alert to improve her methods of teaching, and many opportunities are available. Books written about both men's and women's basketball contain helpful information. Clinics held at many schools and state and regional conventions often present demonstrations of new methods and techniques. Additionally, observing well-played games always is an excellent source for learning more about basketball. Films offer a coach or teacher a chance to see many basketball skills in slow motion, and errors and strategy illustrated. Periodicals often have excellent articles with accompanying illustrations. The Division for Girls and Women's Sports rule book usually contains

1. M. Gladys Scott and Esther French, *Measurement and Evaluation in Physical Education* (Dubuque, Iowa: Wm. C. Brown Company Publishers, 1959), pp. 360 and 367.
2. Ibid., p. 158.

articles for the basketball teacher. Discussing the game with colleagues is one of the best ways of getting information and new ideas. Most people welcome the opportunity to discuss their favorite theories, whether they be the best way to teach a lay-up or how to stop the pivot player.

With all these sources of information available, any teacher can stay abreast of the changes in the game and can find new ways to present skills and plays to her classes or team. She does only half a job, however, if she merely teaches skills and plays. She must also communicate her enthusiasm for the game to her students and make them feel the excitement of play. Women's basketball is a game of speed, skill, deception, endurance, and finesse, and the challenge to put the ball through the basket has never been greater.

REFERENCES

1. Meyer, Margaret, and Schwarz, Marguerite. *Team Sports for Girls and Women.* Philadelphia: W. B. Saunders Co., 1965.
2. Miller, Donna Mae, and Ley, Katherine. *Individual and Team Sports for Women.* Englewood Cliffs, N. J.: Prentice-Hall, Inc., 1955.
3. Neal, Patsy. *Basketball Techniques for Women.* New York: Ronald Press Co., 1966.
4. Newell, Pete, and Benington, John. *Basketball Methods.* New York: Ronald Press Co., 1962.
5. Scott, M. Gladys, and French, Esther. *Measurement and Evaluation in Physical Education.* Dubuque, Iowa: Wm. C. Brown Co., Publishers, 1959.

Suggestions for the Coach

A few easily identifiable requirements are necessary in order that a group of players can form a successful basketball team. These include mastery of fundamental skills, knowledge of offensive and defensive team tactics, and desire to play basketball. Experienced coaches know, however, that sometimes this is not enough. Other less easily definable characteristics such as adaptability, poise, persistence, cooperation, and morale can be strong contributing factors to team success.

How does a coach develop these characteristics in her players? This is not an easily answered question. There are, however, some suggestions which might help a beginning coach.

Preparation in Fundamentals

An obvious recommendation is to provide the best possible preparation in fundamental skills and team tactics. Players who have good backgrounds in basic skills and strategy have the first essential that is required in building a team. Hours of practice on these fundamentals are well worth the time and effort for there is no substitute for them. The development of proficiency is the first step to be taken in establishing confidence and judgment in inexperienced players.

Team Unity

A coach should start building team unity on the first day of practice. She should be specific in explaining what is expected of each team member. This includes the days and time of practices, training rules, scholastic eligibility regulations, method of transportation to games, reporting of injuries or illnesses, medical or parental permissions, desired costume and equipment for practices and games, and any other pertinent information. Regulations should be enforced with fairness and impartiality.

The coach can help cultivate team unity by her attitude toward the substitutes. If a coach indicates by word and action that she feels the substitutes make a valuable contribution, she is instilling in the players not only a feeling of self-worth but also a sense of team responsibility. A coach who shows an interest in only the starting six or seven players can hardly expect the other squad members to have a feeling of team loyalty.

All squad members should be used in practices and the coach should make an effort to see that all players participate in each game. Though this is not always possible, failing to use substitutes after building up a substantial lead is a very discouraging practice to the players on the bench. All team members should be included in strategy sessions, both before and during a game. Substitutes should be expected to join the coach and the players coming to the bench for conference during time outs and intermissions. A loyal group of substitutes can often result in more "desire" for the team on the floor.

Squad meetings or discussions can be very valuable in building team unity and understanding. Theories can be discussed and new tactics presented. If the players are encouraged to ask questions and make suggestions, their understanding of the game will grow proportionally. They should learn to evaluate their mistakes as made against different types of play, and learn to discuss their progression or retrogression objectively. Squad meetings may help build a better understanding of the objectives of the team, a stronger feeling of unity through a common desire, and a closer relationship between the coach and the team.

The captain has the unique position of being the "go between" for the team and the coach. If the coach develops good rapport with the captain, she will have a strong ally. Discussing some of the team problems with the captain may help the coach gain insight about the players and probably will aid the captain in her understanding of the objectives of the coach.

A team that has confidence in the decisions of the coach will be much more enthusiastic about playing than one that secretly prefers another method of play. Though the coach should be careful about putting herself at cross purposes with those of the team, she must remember that the squad has had limited basketball experience and may not be well qualified to judge what is best for the team. The coach must be able to assume the position of authority in both practice sessions and games. If she compromises her beliefs to win the popular support of the players she will probably lose both their respect and support.

Planning Practice

The coach should plan practice sessions carefully. Drills should be explained concisely and should give evidence of preplanning. Including drills which lessen the monotony of practice will help infuse team spirit. Although players should be expected to work hard at practice, the practice should not become drudgery. Competitive drills can be both fun and demanding and variety in drills can keep the practice stimulating and interesting.

The use of pressure situations in practice will aid in the development of poise during games. Pressure can be created in many ways. If the players are doing a warm-up drill such as the grapevine which ends in a lay-up attempt, the players should be instructed to repeat the drill if the lay-up is missed. This means all three players have to run a length of the floor if the basket is not made. Making the basket becomes rather important in this situation. Some of the shooting practice should be done with an opponent lunging toward the shooter. Players must be able to concentrate on the shot attempt regardless of the actions of the opponent. Shooting and passing games can be conducted with points scored for the number of baskets made or passes completed. If the losers of the games have to run a lap, the desire to win becomes greater and the pressure is more intense.

The coach must be careful that she does not build too great a pressure in practice. The learning of new skills and plays should be done in a relaxed atmosphere. However, much of the practice session should be similar to what the players will experience in an actual contest. The use of several players in different positions may tend to keep the players hustling. All players should feel that the coach will give them a chance to work into a starting position.

The coach can help a team prepare for tense and desperate circumstances by creating similar situations in practice sessions. A team should practice playing with 30 seconds remaining and a one point deficit or advantage. Players should experience using and playing against a press in the closing seconds of a game. Special plays for jump balls or out-of-bounds situations can be planned. A team should experience "playing for one"—that is maintaining possession of the ball until the last few seconds and then trying for one basket before the period is over. The best time to attempt the shot is with five or six seconds remaining. This will allow for a second attempt but probably would be inadequate for the opposition to move across the floor to score. Facing these tense situations in practice can help a team to be calm and poised when faced with similar situations in a game.

Planning Schedule

A coach would like to create a schedule that will help her team develop to its fullest potential. If the team is lacking in experience, playing one or two relatively easy teams can do a great deal toward building confidence. All teams like to start the season with a win, and the coach should plan for one of the less difficult opponents, if possible. The coach should try to schedule schools that would provide fairly even competition as no team really enjoys uneven contests.

Sometimes a school has the opportunity to play a team that is considerably out of its class. The coach should give careful consideration to scheduling a contest such as this. There are advantages to playing opponents who can execute plays very skillfully. Players often learn more quickly through their mistakes in a contest than many hours of coaching during practice. If a team has been having a rather successful season, a greater challenge may be very beneficial.

However, absorbing a resounding defeat in public can be very humiliating. A coach should be careful that she does not cause her players to be embarrassed in public. Whether or not she schedules such a game should be decided on the advantages or disadvantages to the students rather than the prestige factor to the school or the number of spectators who will attend.

Other factors besides the skill level of the opponents should be considered in scheduling contests. The distance to travel is an obvious one. The attitude of the players and coach can be a very important factor. Some schools, because of the graciousness of their students and faculty, are highly regarded as opponents and make the game and social hour a pleasant experience. Unfortunately, some schools present a different situation. A team which is rough or unsportsmanlike can make for many unpleasant situations. If the people at a school are

unfriendly or inhospitable, the enjoyment of the game is greatly reduced.

Although a coach would prefer to have the stronger opponents
scheduled in the middle or toward the end of the season, she should
be careful that she does not schedule a series of difficult games. If
a team absorbs three consecutive losses, it may be hard to fight back.
When a team is to be entered in a tournament, the coach would like
for it to be the climax of the season. She should be careful not to
lay too much importance on the outcome of the tournament. A team
may have had a successful season only to lose in the tournament to
a poorer opponent or one previously defeated. Students sometimes lack
perspective of seeing the season as a whole and may be very dis-
heartened about the entire season because of one poorly played game.

Form and Style

Because of the coach's background in basketball and in kinesiology
she will be aware of good patterns of movement in performing basketball skills. She should help the players develop good execution of
skills, but she should be careful in imposing her ideas of style if a
player has developed different habits. The good teacher or coach must
know enough about mechanics of movement that she knows when to
be flexible in allowing her students freedom in determining their movement patterns. The coach needs to develop the ability to analyze movement well and to make fine discernments. The use of movies may help
in this process.

There may be times when a coach feels that she should request a
player to change her movement pattern. This may be very difficult
for the student. The coach should know enough about psychology and
the individual players to know how serious a change in style may
seem to a player. To make a change may be relatively easy for one
player while quite difficult for another. Some factors which might
affect the wisdom of changing would include: how the athlete feels
about changing, the perceptiveness and intelligence of the student,
how much desire for improvement the player has, how much faith
she has in the coach, and how much time is available to effect a change.

The coach will also need to help the players to develop a style of
game play. Some players are very reluctant to shoot while others
seem to want to shoot every time they get the ball. Players should
be encouraged to try the high percentage shot and should come to

know what is a good percentage shot for them individually. The coach needs to develop restraint in a player who loves to shoot. She has to do this without squelching a player and causing her to feel that the coach thinks she is a poor shooter.

The coach will naturally tend to select the players who play her style of game. If she likes the aggressive style of basketball, she will be inclined to play the hustling players. If the coach prefers a more conservative brand of game, she will be apt to choose the more deliberate type of player. The coach must be careful that she does not overlook players with good potential. The wise coach will have a flexible system of play that will be based on the abilities of the players. The skillful coach will be able to blend the skills of the players into a system while molding the available personnel into her style of game.

Substitution

Learning the art of when to substitute is a skill never mastered, but knowing the players well is the first prerequisite. For some players who are having difficulty, a few minutes on the bench may be the answer, but other players may suddenly "catch fire" in the game. If a coach removes a player from the game after she makes one or two mistakes, other players may become tense and nervous for they, too, will anticipate removal. On the other hand, if the coach waits too long she may be hurting the team by allowing a poorly performing player to remain in the game while one of the substitutes might provide the spark that the team needs.

A coach must consider what the team needs in making a substitution: it may be more rebounding strength, a good set shooter or a good ball handler. It is usually wise to replace a player when she has committed her fourth foul. Playing with four fouls can put a great deal of pressure on the player and can have a poor effect on the morale of the team.

It is wise for the coach to have the substitutes who are most likely to enter the game sit by her. With this arrangement the coach can indicate mistakes and situations which occur in the play and help prepare the substitute for the game. When a player leaves the game she should take a seat next to the coach as the coach may want to give her instructions. If outgoing players are expected to sit by the coach, there will be less confusion on the bench.

Time-Outs

The wise use of time-outs is indeed an art. The usual reason for calling a time-out is to plan game strategy. At this time a change in defense or a reorganization of the attack may be discussed. Another common reason for calling a time-out is to stop a sudden burst of scoring by the opponents. It may be necessary to give some advice to the defense or it may merely be hoped that stopping the game will break the scoring spurt of the opponents. Sometimes a time-out is called just to help settle a nervous team or to rest a player. Teams should be careful not to call too many time-outs early in the game for it is best to have one or two remaining for the last few minutes of play.

Developing Desire

Some players have difficulty in making an all-out effort while others have developed a strong competitive urge and respond readily to any challenge. Part of the task of the coach is to develop in each player the desire to do her best. A coach should help the team to prize the satisfaction that may come from having played a good game regardless of the scoring outcome.

If a team plays one or two weak opponents it sometimes becomes complacent because of easy victory and becomes satisfied with a rather mediocre performance. A team will never be very successful unless it has learned to strive for an all-out effort. A team with this type of desire will play more consistently than the one which hopes only to stay ahead of the opposition. Playing strong teams offers much more of a challenge than playing a schedule of weak opponents. Although the coach may anticipate an easy game, she must learn never to underestimate an opponent. An overconfident team is ready for an upset. A wise coach will help the team prepare for a strong opponent, for to expect an easy game is to invite disaster.

Scouting of Opponents

Having advance information about an opponent can be of great value. The person who does the scouting should watch for the total picture of team play as well as keeping statistics and getting exact information. The information should be put in writing and may be of value in succeeding years. Coaching styles often remain the same.

Watching the pregame warm-up can be very helpful as players can be identified and styles of shooting can be observed. The scouting report should include information about individual players and their movements as well as team patterns of offensive and defensive plays. If the second teams are playing a preliminary game, the game should be observed if the same coach works with both teams. A coach often uses similar types of play.

This information should be available in time for the team to devote one or two practices in preparation for the game. This preparation provides for a better educational experience, as the players will have a chance to practice against the opponents' style of play. The team should be able to eliminate some of the trial and error approach when it knows what to expect from the opposition. The use of scouting reports can have a great psychological value, since the players approach the contest with more confidence.

Student Manager

Women have long tried to capitalize on the leadership possibilities inherent in athletic competition. In many cases the person who assumed the responsibilities of the manager was a member of the squad. This has some drawbacks as the first responsibility of a player should be to her duties as a player rather than manager. Selecting a manager who is not a player provides an opportunity for another student to participate in the athletic program. This nonplayer manager can give her full attention to fulfilling her responsibilities in this capacity.

The manager should be responsible to the coach and for this reason the coach may be the best person to select the manager. However, other systems of selection are possible. The coach should help to make this position seem desirable. This will depend on the prestige of the team and on how much the position seems to be a "flunky" job.

The responsibilities are numerous and would be dependent on the desires of the coach. The manager should help with the keeping of records. She should have the forms and see that all the information is kept as accurately as possible. She may keep statistics at practice sessions depending upon what the coach feels is desirable. On days of home games she should act as a hostess to the visiting team and consider herself the official representative of the school and the coach. She should help with the equipment at practices and for away games. If no trainer is available she may assist with taping at the discretion of the coach. There are numerous ways which she can be useful in practice sessions.

The position of manager should free both the coach and the captain from some of the responsibilities that they would otherwise have to assume. The manager should be made to feel that she is a part of the total team effort and is making a valuable contribution. This position allows an opportunity for a girl or young woman who may have great interest in basketball but limited athletic ability to become a part of the team.

Developing Pride and Confidence

The coach should help cultivate a feeling of pride in the team and in the individual players. Recognition by the coach of good defensive play, percentage shooting, assists, and general floor play helps instill pride of accomplishment. Praise should not be given lightly or it will be meaningless, but a good performance should be commended.

Sometimes a private talk between a player and the coach can be very helpful. Such a talk may help the player develop confidence or aggressiveness. The knowledge that the coach has a personal interest in her and confidence in her ability to improve can be a great motivational factor for a beginning player.

A team must learn to accept success with modesty and defeat with no alibis and recriminations. Although every team wants to win, a loss can sometimes be very beneficial. Losing a game can be a strong motivational force and can produce a greater awareness of team and individual weaknesses. Defeat can bring about a greater understanding of self and one's reaction to challenge and adversity. Poise and confidence cannot be learned from easy success alone; these are nurtured in formidable situations.

Leading By Example

The coach must realize that her attitudes and opinions are reflected by her team members. If she is critical of the decisions of the officials, she should not be surprised if the players indicate this attitude on the floor. The coach must realize that she leads by example. This is true in places other than the gymnasium. The coach must help the players see that as members of a team they represent more than a group of individuals. A school or organization is often judged by the appearance and behavior of a few people. A basketball team should develop pride not only in its play during a game but also in its reputation of general sportsmanship, courtesy, and good manners.

REFERENCES

1. Miller, Kenneth D., and Horky, Rita Jean. *Modern Basketball for Women*. Columbus, Ohio: Charles E. Merrill Co., 1970.
2. Neal, Patsy. *Coaching Methods for Women*. Reading, Massachusetts: Addison-Wesley Publishing Co., 1969.
3. Newell, Pete, and Benington, John. *Basketball Methods*. New York: Ronald Press Co., 1962.
4. Wilkes, Glenn. *Winning Basketball Strategy*. Englewood Cliffs, N. J.: Prentice-Hall, Inc., 1962.
5. Wooden, John R. *Practical Modern Basketball*. New York: Ronald Press Co., 1966.

Glossary
of Strategy Terms

Assist—A pass which sets up a basket is credited as an assist. The pass must have created the shooting opportunity, passing around the outside of a zone would not be considered an assist. The basket must be made for the assist to be counted.

Backcourt—The backcourt is that half of the court which contains the opponent's basket.

Backdoor Play—An offensive player makes an outside cut to the basket.

Ball Control—Ball control is a type of offensive play which uses deliberate moving of the ball to obtain a good shot.

Block—A player uses her body to legally obstruct an opponent.

Break—(same as cut).

Buttonhook—The buttonhook is an offensive maneuver by a player without the ball. The player cuts away from the ball and then reverses and comes back toward the ball.

Clear Out—An offensive player vacates an area to make a space for her teammate to maneuver.

Cut—An offensive player without the ball makes a sudden movement into a space.

Defensive Play—Defensive play is any action of a team or an individual when the opponents are in possession of the ball.

Double Pivot—An offensive pattern using two pivot players is called a double pivot.

Double Post—(same as double pivot).

Double Team—Two defensive players converge on one opponent and try to tie the ball or force a bad pass.

Drive—A player makes a sudden move toward an opening by dribbling the ball.

Fake—(same as feint).

Fast Break—The team that has possession of the ball in its own backcourt moves the ball as quickly as possible toward its basket in the hope of getting a short shot before the opponents organize their defense.

Feint—A feint is a pretense to move the ball or the body in order to deceive the opponent and make her move.

Freeze—(same as stall).

Frontcourt—The frontcourt is the half of the court which contains the team's own basket.

Full Court Press—The defensive team attempts to extend its defensive action to cover the entire court.

Give-and-Go—A player passes to a teammate and cuts into a space for a return pass.

Half Court Press—The defensive team spreads its defense to cover the entire backcourt.

High Post—The pivot player operates from a position at the free throw line.

Jump Switch—The jump switch is a defensive maneuver used in pressure situations. In switching defensive assignments the player jumps aggressively forward attempting to thwart the movement of the opponent.

Low Post—The pivot player plays from a position in the lane which is less than 15 feet from the basket.

Man-to-Man Defense—(same as player-to-player defense).

Mismatch—A mismatch is an unequal pairing of opposing players, such as a short defensive player guarding a tall opponent.

Offensive Play—Offensive play is any action of the team or player on the team with the ball.

Overloading a Zone—The offensive team positions two players in a zone covered by one defensive player.

Overplay—An overplay is a defensive adjustment to counteract the strength of the opposition. When guarding a player who always drives the same way, the defensive player should forsake her orthodox position and move to the side of the expected drive.

Pick—The pick is a screen by which a player with the ball drives around a stationary teammate to lose her guard.

Pivot Guard—The pivot guard is the player guarding the pivot.

Pivot Player—A pivot player is an offensive player who plays in the lane and becomes the spearhead of the attack. Many plays start with a pass to the pivot player and a cut. The offensive play could be said to revolve around the pivot player who should be a shooter as well as a passer.

Player-to-Player Defense—Each defensive player is assigned to guard an opponent, and she takes her defensive position in relation to the position of her opponent.

Post Guard—(same as pivot guard).

Post Player—(same as pivot player).

Press—The press is a type of pressure defense which covers a predetermined area of the court and attempts to force the opponents into making mistakes.

Roll—The roll is an offensive maneuver usually executed by a player without the ball in an effort to evade an opponent.

Screen—A screen is an offensive technique used to block the desired movement of an opponent. It is used to free a teammate.

Stall—The offensive team attempts to control the ball but makes no effort to score. The team attempts to maintain possession of the ball in order to prevent the opponents from scoring.

Strong Side—The side of the play with the ball is the strong side. The other side is called the weak side.

Touchdown Pass—A pass in which the receiver is moving away from the passer and catches the ball over her head, as a pass receiver in football does, is called a touchdown pass.

Turnover—The offensive team gives up possession of the ball without an attempted shot.

Two Time—(same as double team).

Weak Side—The side of the play without the ball is the weak side. The other side is called the strong side.

Weave—The weave is a type of offensive play designed to pull the guards away from the basket or to lull them into complacency by repeating the same pattern over and over.

Wing—This term is sometimes given to an offensive player who plays at the sideline such as in a 1-3-1 offensive alignment.

Zone Defense—This is a theory of defense in which the players assume positions in relation to the position of the ball.

Index

positioning, defensive, 11, 112
post, 129
practice session, 120
press, 71-77, 113, 129

rebounding, 15, 74-75, 103, 111
reverse turn, 40
rocker step, 44
roll, 49-50, 88, 90-92, 113, 129

scheduling, 121
scouting, 124
screen, 13, 45-48, 88-92, 112, 129
shooting, 27
    chest, 32, 111
    free throw, 37, 111
    hook, 35, 112
    jump, 33, 113
    lay-up, 29, 111
    one hand push, 31, 111
    two hand overhead, 33, 113
shot chart, 116
stack offense, 105-106

stall, 59, 96, 129
student manager, 125
substitution, 123

team unity, 118
tests
    jump and reach, 116
    thirty-second shooting, 116
time-out, 124
touchdown pass, 94, 102, 114, 130
turnover, 130
two time, 57, 130

units of instruction, 111

weave, 94, 103, 130
wing, 105, 130

zone defense, 59-71, 82, 100-101, 107, 110, 112-113
zone press, 76